Hands-On Agile Software Development with JIRA

Design and manage software projects using
the Agile methodology

David Harned

BIRMINGHAM - MUMBAI

Hands-On Agile Software Development with JIRA

Commissioning Editor: Pavan Ramchandani
Acquisition Editor: Shriram Shekhar
Content Development Editor: Manjusha Mantri
Technical Editor: Abhishek Sharma
Copy Editor: Safis Editing
Project Coordinator: Prajakta Naik
Proofreader: Safis Editing
Indexer: Aishwarya Gangawane
Graphics: Jisha Chirayil
Production Coordinator: Aparna Bhagat

First published: July 2018

Production reference: 2040319

Published by Packt Publishing Ltd.
Livery Place
35 Livery Street
Birmingham
B3 2PB, UK.

ISBN 978-1-78953-213-5

www.packtpub.com

This book is dedicated to my wife, Stephanie, and to my children, Lily and Parker. They help me manage our "project: family" every day. It is the most important, challenging, and rewarding experience.

`mapt.io`

Mapt is an online digital library that gives you full access to over 5,000 books and videos, as well as industry leading tools to help you plan your personal development and advance your career. For more information, please visit our website.

Why subscribe?

- Spend less time learning and more time coding with practical eBooks and Videos from over 4,000 industry professionals

- Improve your learning with Skill Plans built especially for you

- Get a free eBook or video every month

- Mapt is fully searchable

- Copy and paste, print, and bookmark content

PacktPub.com

Did you know that Packt offers eBook versions of every book published, with PDF and ePub files available? You can upgrade to the eBook version at `www.PacktPub.com` and as a print book customer, you are entitled to a discount on the eBook copy. Get in touch with us at `service@packtpub.com` for more details.

At `www.PacktPub.com`, you can also read a collection of free technical articles, sign up for a range of free newsletters, and receive exclusive discounts and offers on Packt books and eBooks.

Contributor

About the author

David Harned is a PMO director for Monotype and is a motivated and inspired leader of Agile thinkers. He is a design, usability, and customer experience advocate. David is an Agile believer and uses Scrum, Kanban, and Lean as well as hybrid approaches for project management. He holds many certifications in the project management and Agile domains, including PMI Project Management Professional, Digital Project Manager, Certified ScrumMaster, and more.

I'd like to thank my former manager, Chris Roberts, without whom I would never have stepped into this field. He made it possible for me to get where I am through his support. Also, I'd like to thank all the other Agile thinkers I have worked with in my teams. They have enriched my thought patterns while making sure I never forgot how to be humble.

Packt is searching for authors like you

If you're interested in becoming an author for Packt, please visit authors.packtpub.com and apply today. We have worked with thousands of developers and tech professionals, just like you, to help them share their insight with the global tech community. You can make a general application, apply for a specific hot topic that we are recruiting an author for, or submit your own idea.

Table of Contents

Preface

JIRA is an Agile project management tool that supports any Agile methodology. From Agile boards to reports, you can plan, track, and manage all your Agile software development projects with a single tool. With this book, you will explore critical Agile terminologies and concepts in the context of JIRA.

Who this book is for

If you want to get started with JIRA and learn how to run your JIRA projects the Agile way, this is the perfect book for you.

What this book covers

Chapter 1, *Getting Started with Creating Projects*, is about getting setting up your first JIRA project. We'll talk about why JIRA is so popular and where it came from. We'll also talk about creating an account with Atlassian so that you can get started using JIRA in the cloud. We'll look into the projects themselves and how we use a project to organize all work items. We'll then look into screens, workflows, and permissions, which will allow us to customize our project, and the views, notifications, and permissions that go along with it.

Chapter 2, *Managing Work Items*, is all about the difference between epics, stories, bugs, and tasks; learning what the different types of issues are, and why we would use each one. We'll talk about the attributes for those issues, learning what these different work item attributes are and how to customize them to fit your needs. We'll also cover managing items of work to create a backlog in JIRA and how to define, prioritize, and refine it. Then, we'll talk about creating and configuring a board and how you would do that.

Chapter 3, *Running Your Project in JIRA*, is about running the project. We'll create and start a Sprint. We'll use our backlog to refine the work and then plan and begin the Sprint iteration. We'll also look at the daily Scrum and how we use JIRA to keep the team aligned, and how to know whether we're on track to meet our commitments. We'll focus on the differences between smaller stories or tasks, and when to use each one. Then we'll talk about how to close a Sprint, and learn how to end that Sprint, and what to do with any work that hasn't been completed.

Chapter 4, *Working with Reports*, explores all about versions and releases—what they are and how they're different from each other. We'll talk about burndowns, about Sprint reports, and how to read them to determine whether or not your team is doing well. We'll also take a look at velocity charts, which we can use to determine the performance of the team. We will take a look at release and epic burndowns, as well as versions and epic reports, which give you the ability to do forecasting, which is very powerful.

Chapter 5, *Issue Searching and Filtering*, is about JQL: what it is, how to write queries in JIRA using simple and advanced editors, and how to export your results. We'll talk about saving and managing filters, and then executing bulk changes, and then how to use those filters to create new boards. This will give you new views of your work items in JIRA.

Chapter 6, *Dashboards and Widgets*, teaches us what a dashboard is, how you would use it, the different things you can put on a dashboard, the different layouts you can have for it, and then how to share it so that you can ensure that you're able to broadcast the results of the team and how things are going.

To get the most out of this book

There aren't a lot of prerequisites for this book; just a couple of things that I thought would be helpful. First, you should have a basic knowledge of Scrum. We'll reference Scrum a fair amount as we're running an Agile project in JIRA, and I'll give you some helpful specifics. Second, it is nice to have at least one team of people that are looking to work together, because that's what JIRA is really great for: having a team of people work together instead of just one person working on something. Although you can use JIRA alone, having a team that you can apply these concepts to once you've learned them will be really powerful.

You will need to be familiar with the basics of JIRA, from both the end-user and administrator perspectives. Experience with workflows, custom fields, and other administrative JIRA functions will be useful.

Download the color images

We also provide a PDF file that has color images of the screenshots/diagrams used in this book. You can download it here: https://www.packtpub.com/sites/default/files/downloads/HandsOnAgileSoftwareDevelopmentwithJIRA_ColorImages.pdf.

Conventions used

There are a number of text conventions used throughout this book.

`CodeInText`: Indicates code words in text, database table names, folder names, filenames, file extensions, pathnames, dummy URLs, user input, and Twitter handles. Here is an example: "Let's create another Sprint. We'll call this one `FP1 Sprint 1` and include `This is my first Sprint` as the Sprint goal."

Bold: Indicates a new term, an important word, or words that you see on screen. For example, words in menus or dialog boxes appear in the text like this. Here is an example: "If we go back to our **Backlog** in the upper right corner, we can see that we have our **Board settings**, so we'll click that, and then, under our **SETTINGS**, we've got **Estimation**."

Warnings or important notes appear like this.

Tips and tricks appear like this.

Get in touch

Feedback from our readers is always welcome.

General feedback: Email `feedback@packtpub.com` and mention the book title in the subject of your message. If you have questions about any aspect of this book, please email us at `questions@packtpub.com`.

Errata: Although we have taken every care to ensure the accuracy of our content, mistakes do happen. If you have found a mistake in this book, we would be grateful if you would report this to us. Please visit `www.packtpub.com/submit-errata`, selecting your book, clicking on the Errata Submission Form link, and entering the details.

Piracy: If you come across any illegal copies of our works in any form on the Internet, we would be grateful if you would provide us with the location address or website name. Please contact us at `copyright@packtpub.com` with a link to the material.

If you are interested in becoming an author: If there is a topic that you have expertise in and you are interested in either writing or contributing to a book, please visit `authors.packtpub.com`.

Reviews

Please leave a review. Once you have read and used this book, why not leave a review on the site that you purchased it from? Potential readers can then see and use your unbiased opinion to make purchase decisions, we at Packt can understand what you think about our products, and our authors can see your feedback on their book. Thank you!

For more information about Packt, please visit `packtpub.com`.

Getting Started with Creating Projects

1

In this chapter, you'll learn about JIRA—what it is, and how it can be used to manage all of the work that you need to do. We'll take a look at how projects can help to keep our work organized in JIRA, and we'll cover some of the options that we have when setting the projects up. Let's get started.

In this chapter, you will learn about the following topics:

- An introduction to JIRA
- Creating an account with Atlassian
- Project creation and management
- How to set up a project using a scheme, screens, workflows, and permissions

Introduction to JIRA

This section will cover the JIRA software essentials. In this section, you will learn about what JIRA is, how to get started with creating projects, and how JIRA organizes the work items within the software.

What is JIRA?

JIRA has been around for a while; originally, it was an issue ticketing system (a bug tracking kind of software). Project management has evolved over the years, and agile processes have become increasingly more popular, so JIRA has evolved into a very effective agile project management tool for both Scrum and Kanban. It is now very powerful in that regard.

JIRA currently offers three different packages, as follows:

- JIRA Core
- JIRA Software
- JIRA Service Desk

JIRA has a huge community, with lots of add-ons that allow for planning, tracking, releasing, and reporting; this gives us even more functionality than what we'd get out of the box. You can learn more about JIRA at `https://www.atlassian.com/software/jira`.

Creating an account with Atlassian

In this section, you'll learn how to create an account, and how to set up your JIRA software so that you can begin to use it for project management:

1. Open the **Atlassian** website. You'll see that there's plenty of information about the company, some of the different software products that they have, and more. We'll go to the **Try free** button at the top of the page:

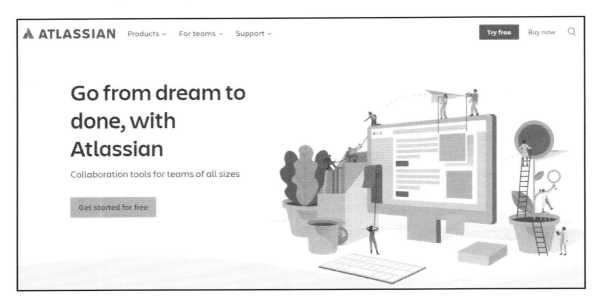

2. You'll see that there are some options. We're going to use **Jira Software**. There is a server version and a cloud version:

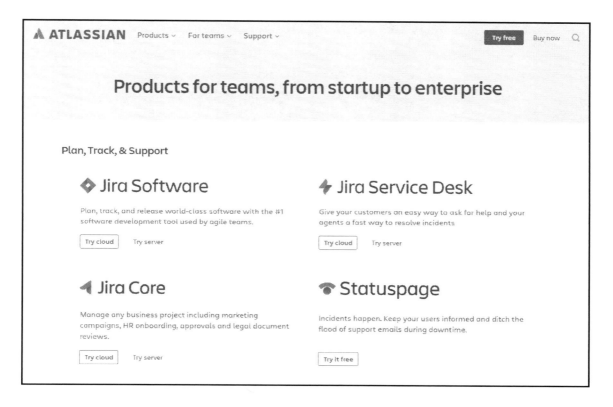

3. We're going to be using the cloud version, so let's select that. We can try it for free for seven days, and there will be some different options for it once it becomes a paid subscription. Since we're just a small team, we'll go ahead and take the first option, which is **$10/month**, and we will **Try it free**:

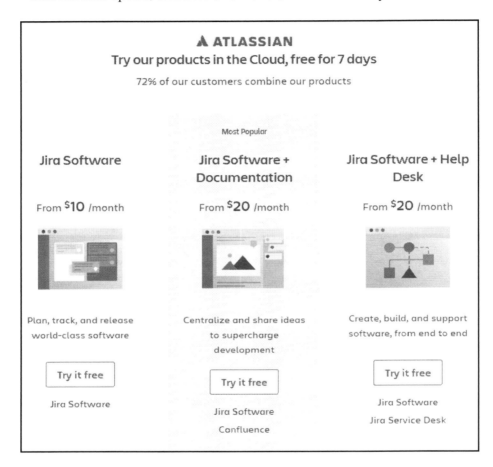

4. On the following screen, we will be asked to go ahead and set up our URL. We'll choose `digitalcoffeetest`, and put in our **Full name** and **Email**, then add a **Password**:

Once we've done that, the website will go ahead and send us an email to validate the data that we just gave them. Once we check our email and validate that the information is correct, we can then go back to the site and log in.

All set! Creating an account is that easy.

How JIRA uses projects to keep work organized

Follow these steps to create projects in JIRA:

1. Log in using our JIRA credentials. Click on **Create project**:

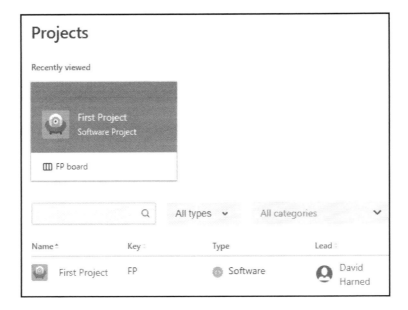

Projects view

2. I have already created a **First Project**, so in our example, let's name the project Second Project. In the following screenshot, you can see that we have a **Scrum** template, and we can change that to something else if we want to; for now, we'll leave it as it is and click on the **Create** button:

3. Now, as you can see in the following screenshot, we have a **First Project**, as well as our new **Second Project**:

4. Go to **View all projects**, where you will be able to see all of the projects, as follows:

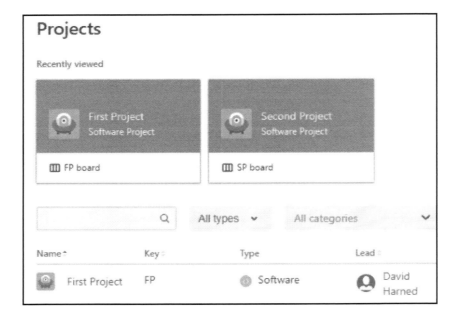

5. Click on **Second Project.** In the following screenshot, you can see what the **Backlog** view looks like. This is where we can create a test story and put items into our backlog:

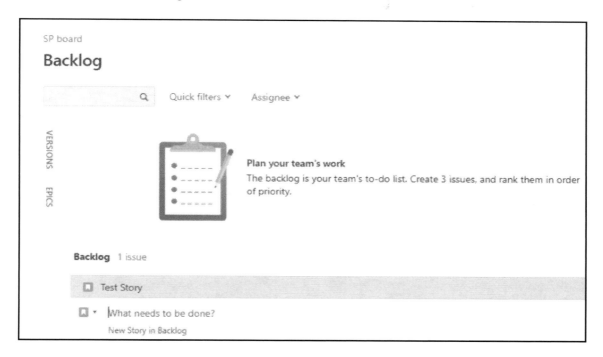

JIRA uses projects to help us organize our work and create a holding place for everything. Each project has a unique key, which is a three- or four-digit ID that we can reference, as well. You'll see those more as we move forward in this book.

We'll go into more detail about what all of these different things are in the UI, but for now, it's important to note that projects are what JIRA uses in order to organize our work.

Project management

In this section, we'll discuss managing projects in JIRA.

The steps for managing projects in JIRA are as follows:

1. Select **Projects** in the left-hand menu. You will see a **First Project** and a **Second Project**:

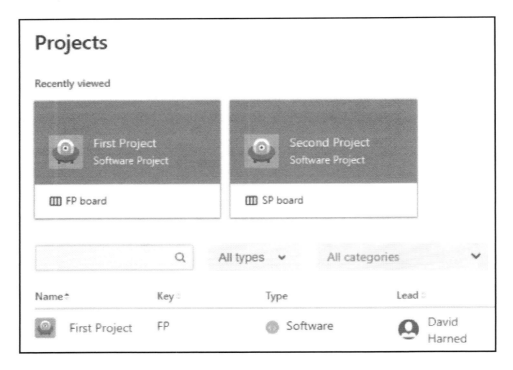

2. Select the **First Project**. This will bring you to the **Backlog** view of the project. The backlog is where we will store all of the stories, bugs, and different work item issue types that we want inside of this project:

Backlog view of the project

In the **Backlog** view, you'll see some options. First, there is a search option. To start a search, we just start to type in the box, and the backlog will filter itself to match what is typed. There are also some drop-down options, named **Quick filters** and **Assignee**. These allow us to filter the contents of the backlog, to quickly refine it to whatever we choose.

In the left-hand column, you will also see the following options:

- **Active sprints**: We can select this and get the board view for the current sprint.
- **Reports**: These are all of the reports that we can look at for this project.
- **Releases**: This is where we batch up a large amount of value into a version and release it; this lets us look at all of the details of each release, including what's in it and where we are in the process of building it.
- **Issues and filters**: This lets us write queries to search for work items, and then save them as filters.
- **Components**: These are groups of work items that we can customize and use to manage the work items.

3. Go down to **Project settings**. This will take you to the following screen:

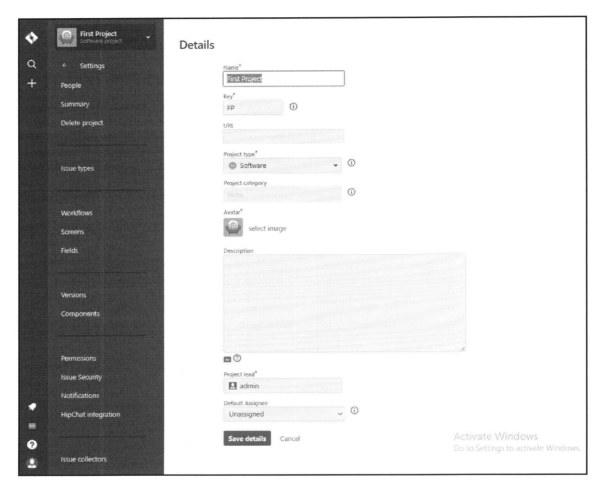

Project Settings

As you can see, we have our project **Name**, a unique **Key**, a **URL**, and the **Project type**; we're going to stick with the **Software** type, so that we can use agile processes, like Scrum. We can categorize this project, we can select an **Avatar** image, and we can write a **Description**. We can also decide who the **Project lead** will be on this project (**admin**), and we can decide whether a new item created in the backlog will get assigned to the **Project lead** (**Default Assignee**), which in this case, would be the admin; or, we can even leave it **Unassigned**.

There are a lot of options on the left-hand side of this **Project settings** page, but we're going to take a look at the **Summary** view, because the summary is going to give us a look at all of those different options in one view. **Issue types** and **Workflows** are shown in the following screenshot:

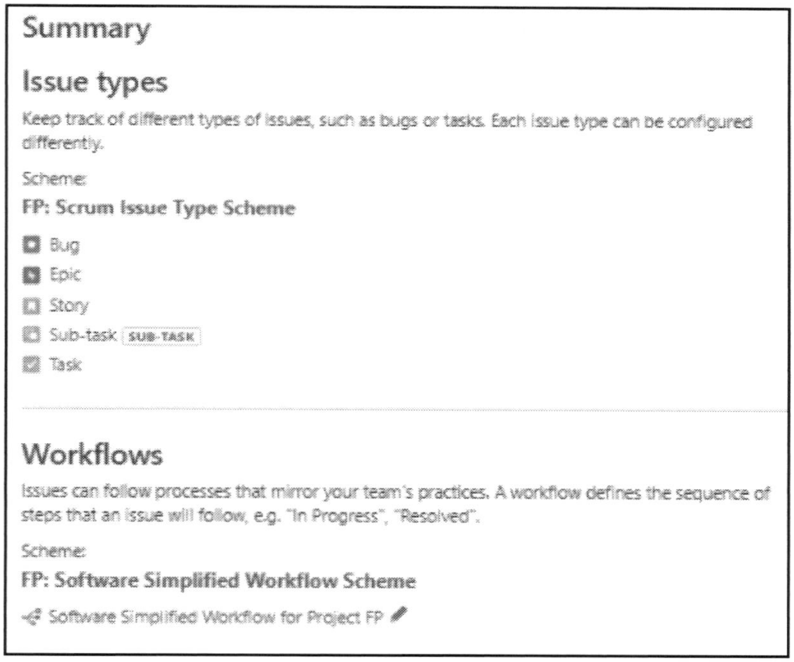

Summary

Issue types

Keep track of different types of issues, such as bugs or tasks. Each issue type can be configured differently.

Scheme:
FP: Scrum Issue Type Scheme

- Bug
- Epic
- Story
- Sub-task SUB-TASK
- Task

Workflows

Issues can follow processes that mirror your team's practices. A workflow defines the sequence of steps that an issue will follow, e.g. "In Progress", "Resolved".

Scheme:
FP: Software Simplified Workflow Scheme

Software Simplified Workflow for Project FP

Summary of Project Settings

Summary of project settings

Before we dive deeper into all of the project settings, let's take a high-level look. First, let's take a look at **Workflows** so that we can understand how workflows operate. We'll go into more detail in the next section, but what you really need to understand is that this will control the way that the issues move from **To Do**, to **In Progress**, to **Done**, and that we can customize the way that they work:

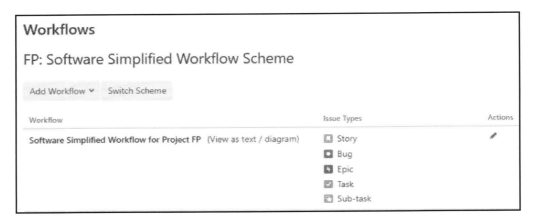

Workflows configuration

If we take a look at the **Screens** for this project, we can see that we're using a **Scrum Issue Type Screen Scheme**. The **Screens** allow us to select the attributes that appear on the different issue types, such as the story points, assignee, and acceptance criteria:

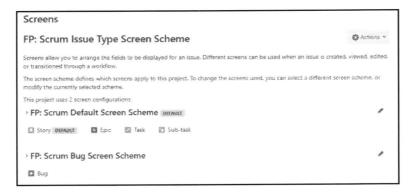

Screens configuration

Now, look at the **Fields**. This allows you to control the fields that are available:

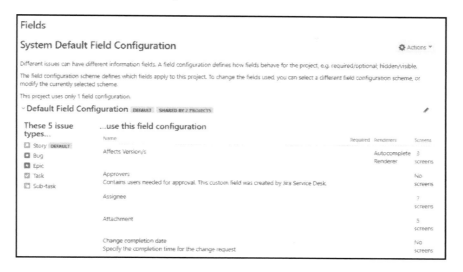

Fields configuration

You can also do things like set up and create components. Components are similar to the concept of a tag, which allows us to search or filter work items.

If you'd like to try to create one, you can click on **Components** on the left-hand side, and call this component `Test`:

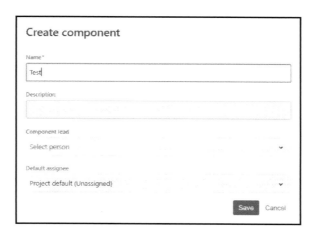

Creating a component

You can also do things such as setting permissions for software projects, as shown in the following screenshot:

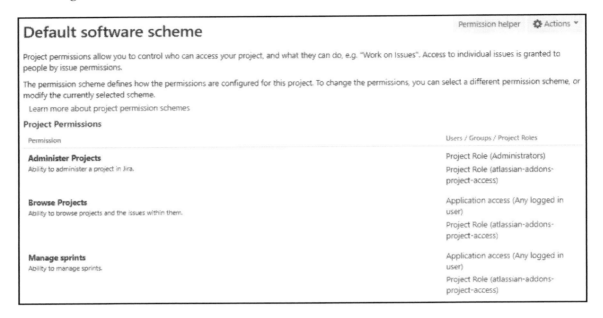

Permission schemes are editable

You can even set a scheme for **Notifications**, as follows:

Notifications

Default Notification Scheme
SHARED BY 2 PROJECTS

Jira can notify the appropriate people of particular events in your project, e.g. "Issue Commented". You can choose specific people, groups, or roles to receive notifications.

The notification scheme defines how the notifications are configured for this project. To change the notifications, you can select a different notification scheme, or modify the currently selected scheme.

- Email: jira@▨▨▨▨▨▨▨.atlassian.net ✎

Events	Notifications
Issue Created	All Watchers
	Current Assignee
	Reporter
Issue Updated	All Watchers
	Current Assignee
	Reporter
Issue Assigned	All Watchers
	Current Assignee
	Reporter

Default Notification scheme

As you can see, when an issue is created, we will notify—**All Watchers**, the **Current Assignee**, and the **Reporter.** We can also customize this. If you're one of those people that receive way too many emails already, you might want to slim this down a little bit, so that you will only be notified about the most important actions.

That concludes our quick look at projects and their settings in JIRA. Now, let's go into some more detail.

How to set up a project using a scheme, screens, workflows, and permissions

In the last section, you learned how to configure schemes in JIRA; we introduced screens, workflows, permissions, and even notifications.

In this section, you will learn about the following topics in detail:

- Screens
- Workflows
- Permissions
- Notifications

Screens

Let's flip over to the JIRA account and look at our project view, as follows:

1. Select the **First Project**, and, once you have the project loaded up, choose the settings for the project. Go over to the left-hand menu and select **Settings**.

2. In the previous section, you saw a little bit about screens, but now, you're going to learn about them more deeply. We use what's called a **Scrum Issue Type Screen Scheme**. We have a **Scrum Default Screen Scheme** that will cover the different work item issue types of **Story**, **Epic**, **Task**, and **Sub-task**; then, we have a **Scrum Bug Screen Scheme** that will cover the issue type **Bug**, as shown in the following screenshot:

Editing the default Scrum Issue Type Screen Scheme

3. Click on the **edit** icon on the right. We can then take a look at the default **Issues** screen, as follows:

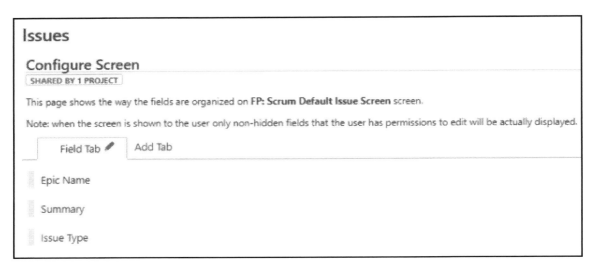

Configuring the screen fields

4. This will give us control over all of the different fields that appear in an issue type. There may be some that we don't need to use, because our organization doesn't use them, or we don't find value in them. In that case, removing them from the interface will make things faster and/or cleaner. We can also drag and move the fields into different orders. Suppose that, for instance, we didn't want **Components**. We could easily just remove that by clicking on **Remove**. The **Components** would then no longer appear on any of our issue types, with the exception of bugs. We haven't configured the bug type yet.

5. At the bottom of the screen, we have the ability to select a field to add, as well; so, we can actually use that to add **Components** back, as follows:

Component/s addition on screen fields

We can just type `components` and add it back that way; we can drag it back up to right above **Description**, where we had it before.

That concludes our discussion of how to use screens in JIRA. Next, let's take a look at workflows.

Workflows

In the options on the left-hand side of the screen, click on **Workflows**.

Adjustments to workflows allow us to see the different ways that a status can interact with another status, and how items can move from one status to the next:

1. Click on **FP: Software Simplified Workflow Scheme**, as shown in the following screenshot:

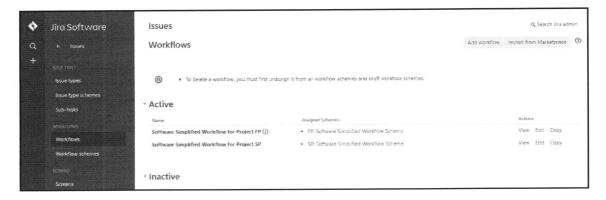

List of Workflows

This will take us to the following screen, which gives us a flow diagram of the workflow:

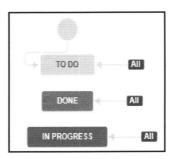

Default Workflow example

2. Any type of work item can be moved to **TO DO** from all other states in the workflow. The same is true for **DONE** and **IN PROGRESS**. This is, by default, a highly accommodating workflow.
3. We can add a new status, such as CLOSED, by clicking on **Add status**.

4. Drag the new **CLOSED** status to the bottom, beneath **IN PROGRESS**; now, we have a new status, as follows:

Adding a CLOSED status to our Workflow

Then, we can create different actions that will happen when work items are moved in and out of this new closed status. For example, if our team is burning down hours as a metric instead of story points in our sprints, we may want to have the remaining hours item update itself to zero when the work item is moved into the **CLOSED** state. Another option would be to set the **Resolution** value of the work item behind the scenes, when we transition the item to closed. These are just a few examples of things that we can do in a workflow.

Permissions

Next, we want to take a look at permissions, so we'll bring up the **Permissions** options for our default software scheme, which is what we're using for our Scrum project, as shown in the following screenshot:

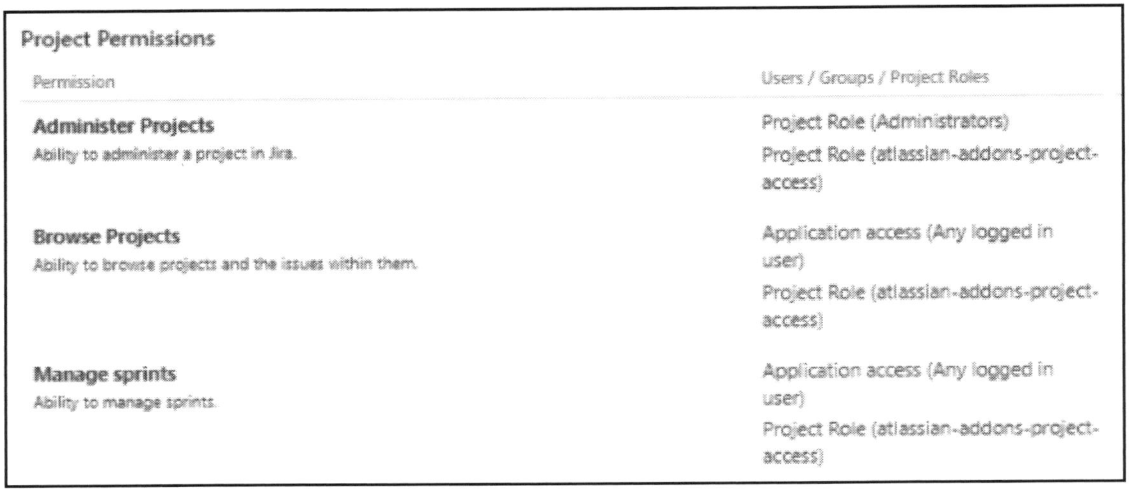

Project Permissions	
Permission	Users / Groups / Project Roles
Administer Projects Ability to administer a project in Jira.	Project Role (Administrators) Project Role (atlassian-addons-project-access)
Browse Projects Ability to browse projects and the issues within them.	Application access (Any logged in user) Project Role (atlassian-addons-project-access)
Manage sprints Ability to manage sprints.	Application access (Any logged in user) Project Role (atlassian-addons-project-access)

Managing permissions and access controls

Since we have access to everything, this isn't really critical right now, but if we'd had more people assigned to this project, then we might have wanted to assign who could do what, from both a project-permissions perspective and an issue-permissions perspective.

Notifications

There is also a **Notifications** option under our **First Project**. You learned a little bit about this in the last section, but you'll learn more about it now:

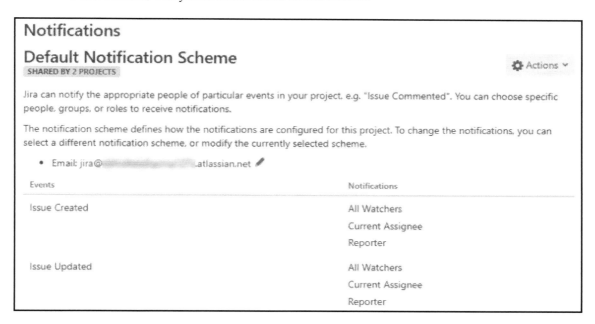

Notifications can be tailored specific to a project

Suppose that you were the person that reported an issue, and, when that issue was created, as the reporter, you would be notified. You would also want the current assignee to be notified, since they have had something assigned to them. You'd also want any of the watchers of that item to be notified. Then, suppose that the issue gets updated. It may be that you (the reporter) don't want to be notified about that. Here, you can configure the notifications and set them up the way you would like.

You can execute the preceding scenario by clicking on **Delete** for the **Reporter**, under the **Issue Updated** section. This will take you to the following screen:

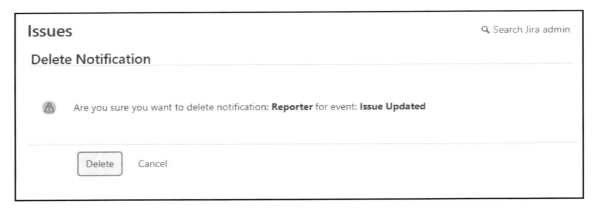

We can add and remove notifications

The reporter will now be notified an item is created, but not when it's updated. The reporter is again notified when the item is assigned.

Summary

We've now reached the end of our first chapter. In this chapter, we discussed what JIRA is, what it's used for in today's project management world, and why we should use it with agile. You learned how to create an account with Atlassian so that you can start to use JIRA. We then discussed projects, and how JIRA organizes its work into projects as containers. We covered creating and managing different projects in JIRA, and how to handle their settings. Finally, you learned more about the specifics in the configuration of projects, such as screens, workflows, permissions, and notifications.

In the next chapter, we'll discuss managing all of the work items in more detail, since there are lots of them involved. JIRA will help us to achieve these goals.

2
Managing Work Items

In the previous chapter, we learned about what JIRA is, how to get started with it, and how to create a project in JIRA. In this chapter, we're going to learn about managing all of the work items that we have.

In this chapter, we'll be learning about epics, stories, bugs, and tasks; what each of these things are; and how we will use and create them in an agile project. Then, we're going to learn about issue type attributes. We're going to talk about adding and removing them, and making them fit the type of work that we're doing in JIRA. Then, we're going to learn about managing the items in our backlog, before learning about our board (those of us that do scrum are going to feel very comfortable with the board) and how to configure it.

In this chapter, we will learn about the following topics:

- Introducing epics, stories, bugs, and tasks
- Issue type attributes and adding and removing them
- Managing items in the backlog
- Creating and configuring our board

Introducing epics, stories, bugs, and tasks

Epics, as you might imagine, are large stories. We want them to be able to be completed, so it's important that they have a distinct start and end, just like any story. We like to think of epics as something that would span multiple sprints, versus a story, which could be completed within a sprint. Epics are not groupings of work items, which is a common mistake that people make when organizing their work in the JIRA interface. We'll take a look at how to use components and labels to do this, instead of epics. Epics will contain stories, bugs, and tasks.

Stories are smaller than epics. Stories, bugs, and tasks are all on the same level hierarchically; they could all be prioritized against one another within our backlog to include in a sprint. Stories are also known as **user stories**, and they're called that because they should focus on delivering value to our users. We need to make sure that we're continuing to think about the people that we're building for. That's why they call them user stories, or stories for short.

Bugs are defects, and they occur when there's a problem. In JIRA, bugs are something that we prioritize against a new feature. We should consider the question, *do we want to take the time in this sprint to fix something, or do we want to create something new?* We should be prioritizing those two things and pitting them against one another as we determine which provides the most value.

A subtask is also something we'll also take a look at. If we have multiple people working on a story or a bug and we want to assign it a more granular level of detail, we can use a subtask to do this.

Creating epics, stories, bugs, and tasks

To learn about epics, let's go to our projects. We created our **First Project** and **Second Project** in the previous chapter.

The following are the necessary steps to create an epic in a project:

1. Click on the **First Project** that we created in our JIRA account.

2. Within our project, we can see that we have the **Backlog** view. In this view, we have three stories. We can see on the left-hand side of the following panel that we have versions and we have epics. Click on **EPICS**:

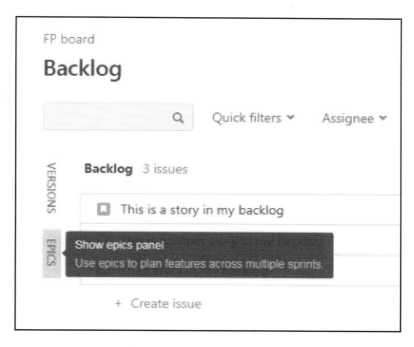

Click to expand the Epics in the Backlog view

3. In the previous screenshot, we can see that we don't have any epics. We'll create an epic and we'll call this epic, `My Test Epic`. In the summary, we can insert information regarding what the epic is about. Let's go ahead and create it. We need a summary, which we'll call `This is a summary`. We now have a test epic:

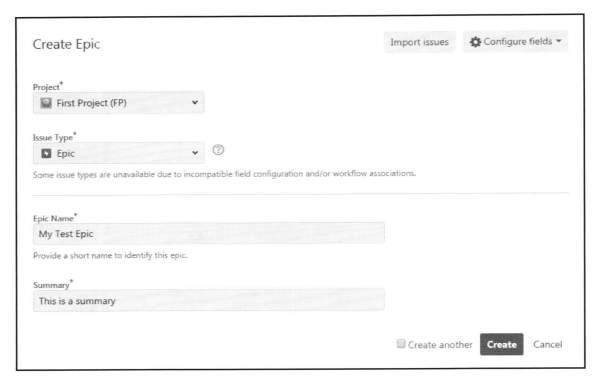

Creating an Epic

Let's take a look at this epic in this screenshot. It has a JIRA ID of **FP-4**; the Key is FP and the 4 is sequential, so this is the fourth item we have created:

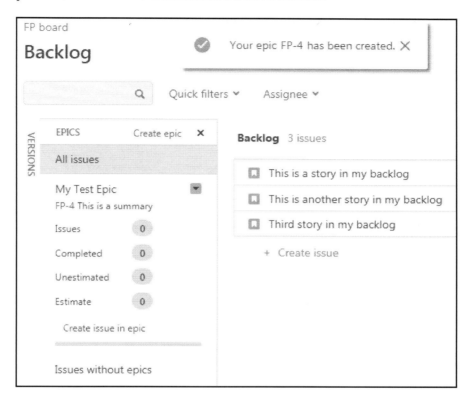

JIRA items are numbered sequentially

In the sub-menu for the epic, we can select the color that we want to use for it, and can edit the name, the epic's details, and mark it as done:

Epics display customization

More importantly, underneath the epic, we can see how many issues or stories, bugs, or tasks are contained within this epic. We can also see how many are completed, unestimated, and how many are estimated. At the bottom, we can see a visual status bar.

We will create our backlog items and then *drag* those on top of our epic—that's how we assign them to the epic. This epic is a story—it's a big story, but it's something that can be started and finished. Your instincts might tell you to group your stories this way with dragging and dropping, but it's important that this is not just a grouping, as that's not the intent of an epic.

If we want to group items in JIRA, we must do something slightly different. For this, what we can do is use components:

1. Select **Components** from the options on the left-hand side.
2. We'll create one component because we don't have one. Let's call this `My Test Component`. We will use the same value in the description. We can select a **Component lead** and also a **Default assignee**, who will basically be the same person that is assigned to the project by default:

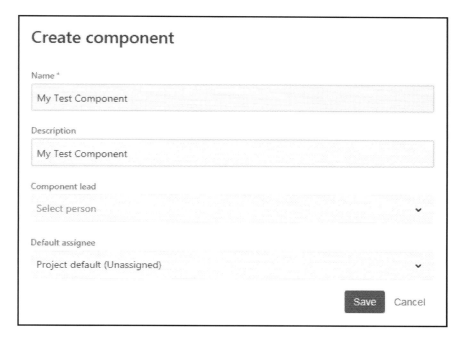

Creating a component

We can use the component that we've created to group items together.

Let's have a look at how to create a story.

We can see that we have three stories. We'll go ahead and create a new one. We'll call this `The newest story`.

We can see when we're creating the stories, that we have the options to create a story, a task, or a bug, and that they're all ranked the same hierarchically within JIRA:

 A story generally represents a piece of new functionality, a task is just something that needs to be done, and a bug is something that's broken that needs to be fixed.

Issue type selection when creating an item

We'll create **The newest story**, create **The newest task**, and then we'll create **The newest bug**, and that way we have all three. We can take a look at them in the following screenshot:

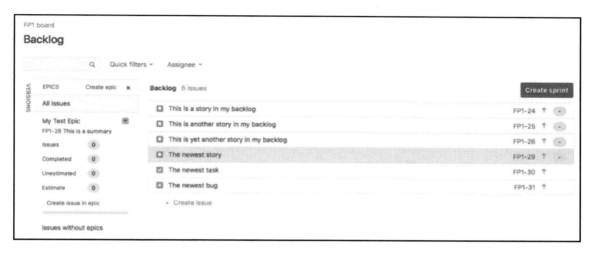

View of the newest story, task, and bug

When we select one of these items, a preview pane on the right-hand side will show us details about it.

When we select an item in this **Backlog** view, we can then press the *E* key on our keyboard, and it will prompt an edit dialog to appear. This is just a nice little shortcut. Another shortcut is as follows: if we select an item and it's unassigned, we can actually hit the *A* button on our keyboard and it will prompt us to assign an item to someone.

The last thing we'll look at in this particular section is how to create a subtask. If we've got our newest story on the preview pane, we can see that we've got the abilities to add an attachment, to link an item, to link to multiple items together and create dependencies, and then we have the create a subtask option:

Creating Subtasks within the Preview Pane

Again, we might use the subtask if this story is going to need to be worked on by multiple people and if we really want to have more granularity around what each person's going to do. We can type in `This is my subtask`, and we can create this subtask by clicking the **Create** button.

Subtasks allow us to use multiple different items of work that exist within a story.

In this section, we learned about epics, stories, bugs, and tasks (and subtasks, too). In the next section, we're going to talk about issue type attributes. We're going to look at each of the different attributes that are available underneath the different issue types in more detail, and then we're going to talk about adding and removing them so that they fit our work better.

Issue type attributes and adding and removing them

In this section, we're going to cover issue type attributes, how to add them, and how to remove them.

First, we're going to learn about what the different kinds of attributes are that can be assigned to stories, tasks, and bugs. Then, we're going to talk more about how we can customize them and adjust the screen so that we can only see the ones that we want to see.

The following are the attributes that are available to us:

- **Assignee**: This is the person that is responsible for that item.
- **Attachments**: These are anything that needs to be attached to that item to provide more clarity or show that it's been done.
- **Comments**: These are used to add our views and feedback or to track progress against the work item.
- **Component/s**: These are groupings, and are used to group items together within a project.
- **Description**: This describes the work that needs to be done for this item to be completed.
- **Epic link**: This is a link to the epic that contains this work item.
- **Fixed version/s**: A version is a large grouping of functionality that is released at once. If the story, bug, or task is part of a version, it would be there.
- **Issue type**: This is a story, bug, or task.

- **Labels**: These are like components, but are a way of grouping work items across projects.
- **Linked issues**: This allows us to create a dependency between different issues if something depends on another work item, or if it's blocked by another work item.
- **Priority**: This is pretty obvious. We can choose from high, medium, or low priority in JIRA.
- **Sprint**: Is the work item contained within a sprint, and if so, which sprint?

Let's take a look at some of these work item attributes:

We've got the newest story that we created earlier. We'll press the *E* key on our keyboard, or we can use the three ellipses in the top right-hand corner to go into edit mode.

We're looking at issue **FP1-29**. This is our newest story. We can see in the following screenshot that as we move down the screen, we've got the ability to change the issue type from **Story** to **Task**, **Bug**, or **Epic**:

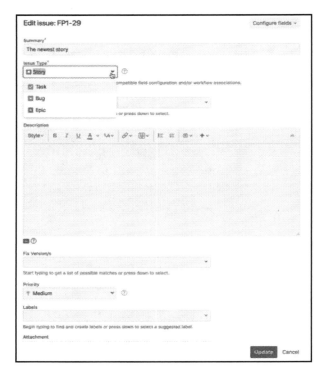

Issue type alteration

In the last section, we created a component. We can actually look for that component here. If we want to use that component on this work item, we've got My test component, which allows us to group this with other similar items:

Grouping of items using components

The **Description** has a rich text editor, which is nice. We've got **Fix Version/s**, which allows us to determine which release this is going to be in. A version is something that we will eventually release. We also have a **Priority** here. **Labels**, which are groupings across projects, are something we can actually look for just by selecting them, and we can also create new ones within the drop-down menu here. If we want to use `cross-project-label` as a label, we can go ahead and assign that label to this work item. We can use **Attachments** by dragging and dropping them in the space provided, or we can browse and upload. In **Linked Issues**, we can link this issue to another issue. There's a variety of ways we can connect items, either by using **blocks**, **is blocked by**, **clones**, **is cloned by**, **duplicates**, and more. Then, we can type in the issue we'd like to link to in here directly, and we can actually perform a search in real time. We can assign this issue to someone else or to ourselves. We can assign the epic, and we can assign what sprint it should appear in (don't forget that we can also assign a work item to epics and sprints by dragging and dropping them in the backlog view):

Creating dependencies between work items

The other thing that we should note here is the **Configure fields** option in the upper-right corner. Sometimes, if we're not going to use a lot of these fields, but still need the data in them, it makes sense to hide them from view without removing them.

If we select the **Configure fields** option, we can see that we have the ability to turn their visibility on and off. We can select the **Custom** option and uncheck the **Comment** field or others. When we save these changes, we'll see that this is the case for the items that we view going forward:

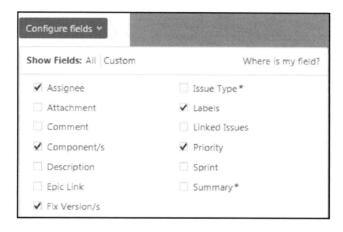

Configure fields

We've also got the ability to watch or unwatch an item:

Preview pane

This is helpful if we have multiple people on our project and we want someone to be notified if the status of this item changes. This is a great way to loop a stakeholder in on a work item that they are asking the status of regularly. We can see that we're a watcher on this item. Even though it's unassigned, the item has been reported by us, which automatically makes us a watcher. Remember our notifications workflow from the previous section that we went through?

Also in the preview pane, we've got our label that we created, we've got a status on this item, the ability to link an item, add an attachment, and the ability to create subtasks. We can also perform a story point assignment. We can look at the components and priority. We can see that this work item contains time-tracking and comments.

We get a lot of functionality in the preview pane, which is really convenient as we don't have to end up leaving the screen to do modifications. Some of these fields, such as story points, will not be editable once we pull them into a sprint. Once this story enters a sprint, we're not going to be able to change some of these values.

In the next section, we're going to talk about managing those items in the backlog. We've got all of these items and we've assigned all of these attributes, so we're going to need to be able to manage them, prioritize them, and more.

Managing items in the backlog

In this section, we're going to learn about managing the items in our backlog.

Here, we will learn about the following:

- How to create items
- How to prioritize items
- How to assign items into epics and versions
- How to create and use quick filters in our board view
- Separating work that's fully refined and ready for a sprint

Let's go back to our backlog and view our work items. It's really easy to prioritize these items in JIRA. All we have to do is drag and drop them in the order we want. This makes it really easy for our product owners to just move all of this stuff around so that it's exactly how they think it should be in order to deliver the most value.

We made an epic previously, and as we can see in the following screenshot, we've got **My Test Epic**. We want to assign some items to this—maybe all of the newest items in the backlog. Let's take the first story (**The newest story**), drag it over to our epic, and once we do that, we'll get a message that it has been added to the epic. We can also see that we now have an issue assigned in our epic:

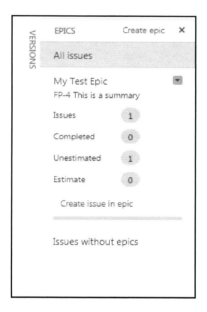

Total issues and their status is visible in the Backlog Epic view

Let's go ahead and take the bug and the task and move these items over as well, so that we have three items in our epic. We select multiple items by just holding down the *Shift* key:

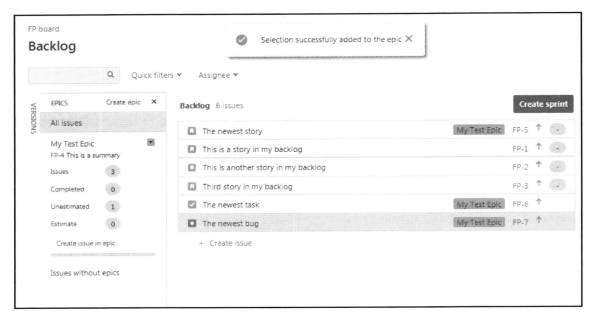

Adding items to the Epic

Next, we've got what're called versions. Versions are an increment of value that we can release to either our customers, our market, or to something similar. In some cases, we might use versions as a way to track the amount of work that's been completed in a month or some other increment of time:

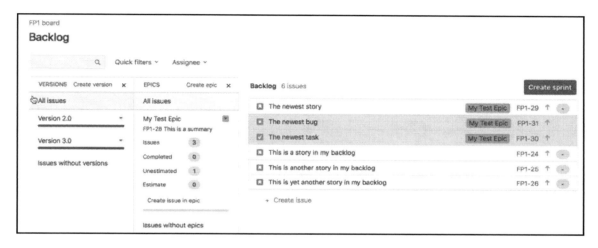

Managing items in the backlog

A version is a little bit different compared to an epic. We may have multiple epics inside a version, or we may just have one epic inside a version. We can see in the preceding screenshot that we have links to issues without versions, and issues without epics. These two may be related, but they're also not necessarily hierarchically connected. A version is a way for us to group work together and, as we can see, if we take a look at **Releases**, ultimately a version is something that we're going to release. As we can see in the following screenshot, we have version 2 and 3, which are unreleased:

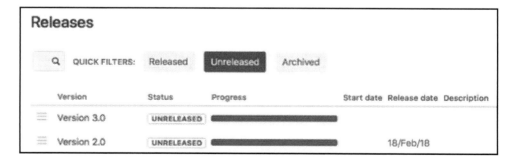

View of the unreleased versions

We can select these items and can take a look at the items that appear within them. In this example, I took all of the default items that were in JIRA when we created this project and put them in **Version 2.0**:

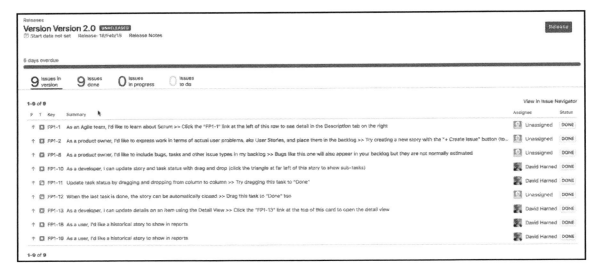

Issues in Version 2.0

We can see that this gives us a nice view of things that are in the version, how much has been done, and how much is in progress. You'll see when we get to the reports section that we can also forecast with versions. Once a version is complete, we can hit the **Release** button, and we can release this version. All of these capabilities are what makes a version so powerful.

Going back to our backlog again, just like the epic, it's fairly easy to take the items and assign them to a version. We can see that we've got some visual confirmation that these are in an epic. If we drag them over and put them inside a version, we're going to get that, too. We can see that this is contained inside version 2, and we can take the other two versions and do the same thing. The stories are in version 2, and they're also part of this epic:

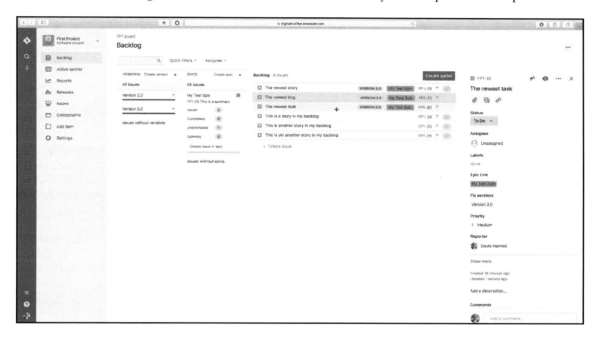

Single screen access to versions, epics, and stories in the backlog view

Next, we want to take a look at **Quick filters**. These can be really powerful, especially if we're working together with our team and we've got to be looking at this backlog and moving quickly through the items in it. JIRA gives us some default quick filters. They only give us issues and items that have been updated recently. They also give us **Assignee**, which is also helpful, but let's say we want to take a look at anything that would be part of the component that we assigned earlier:

Viewing the Backlog by Assignee

Do you remember that we created a component called **My Test Component** earlier? We're going to go to the top corner of the **Backlog** screen and select **Board settings**, and then use that component we made as a filter. Don't worry—we'll take a look at a lot of these board settings later in the next section.

We're going to go under **Quick Filters** and call this component, `Test Component`. In our query for this filter, our **JQL** is going to be `component= "My Test Component"` to match the name we gave the component we created and assigned. We can also put a description if we want to. Next, we'll hit the **Add** button, and we'll have created a quick filter called `Test Component`:

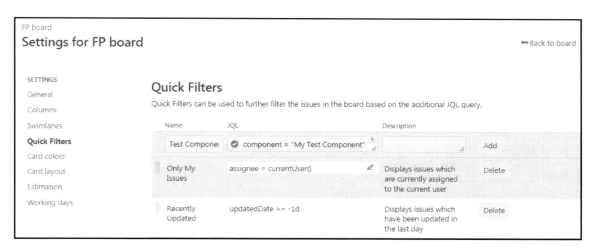

Setting up Quick Filters on our board

When we return to the **Backlog** again, we will see that we have a **Test Component** query in our **Quick Filters** list. If we select this, only the items that have that component assigned to them will appear. We assigned that component as **My Test Component** earlier to the newest story when we were in the **Edit** window for that story, so that it appears here in the filtered view:

The next thing we want to take a look at is the creation of what I call a **ready** sprint. Click on **Clear all filters** so that we can see all of our items again. By clicking the **Create sprint** button, we can create a sprint. We're not going to run it yet, but we can use that as a container to help us when we have work in our backlog that's ready to go. We call that *refined*. We've got work here that's refined, and it meets our *definition of ready* for the team, and it can also come into a sprint. This means that it should have acceptance criteria, it will be sized with some sort of a value, and it will have all the information required for us to fix or build something:

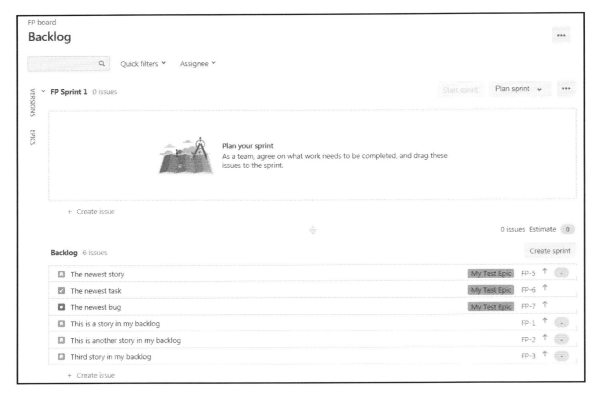

Creating a sprint

We can take the three newest items, as shown in the following screenshot, and we can drag them straight up and place them into the sprint we created. Click the three ellipses and edit this sprint. We will call this sprint `Ready`:

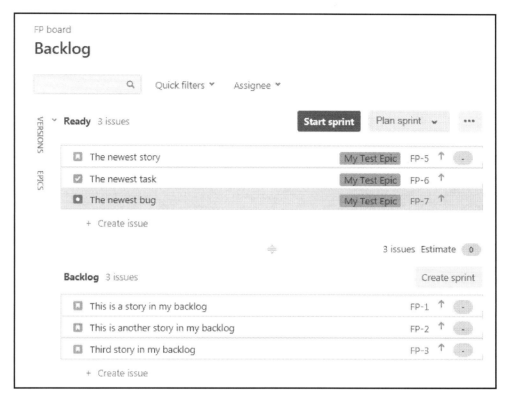

Creating a Ready sprint to hold our refined work

Then, we can use that fully refined work, not only in our next sprint, but as the team increases in velocity, to actually pull stories from this section into our sprint so that the team has work as they accelerate. We'll look more at that as we get into running a sprint.

In the next section, we're going to talk about creating and configuring the board. We've got our backlog ready to go, we've got issues that have been created, and they've been assigned into epics and versions. We know what all of the attributes are underneath those things.

Next, we're going to take a look at the board, which is what we're going to use when we're running a sprint, which means that we're preparing to run our first sprint.

Creating and configuring our board

In this section, we're going to learn how to create and configure our board, and so we're going to talk about the following:

- The differences between a virtual scrum board and an actual scrum board
- The columns that represent workflow states, and how to modify a workflow
- Swimlanes
- Estimation options – time versus story points

Let's go ahead and go over to JIRA. We can see that we've actually taken the backlog items that were not in our ready sprint and pulled them into **Sprint 0**. This will eventually be the sprint that we'll put on our sprint board, but in the meantime, we have to get our board ready. In preparation for our sprint, we've assigned story point values to each of these stories. It is very important that we assign the sizing *before we start a sprint*, as it will represent the commitment.

We are able to see the story point values within the gray oval for each work item, and we can also see them in the preview pane of each item as well:

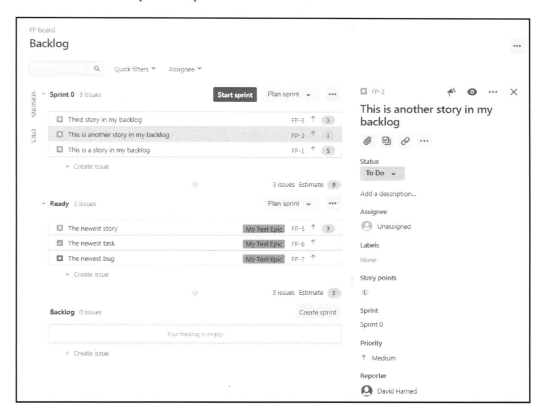

Creating Sprint 0 and making sure that work has story points assigned

Available via a link in the left column, the following screenshot represents our **Active sprints**, and this is eventually going to be our board. If we hit **Start sprint**, these items will appear on this active sprint board, but before we do that, let's just take a look at this board.

You may already known that a physical scrum board will be a white board with columns on it. Each one of those columns will represent the different steps in our workflow. Scrum suggests sticky notes, which we can move across these columns. JIRA models this as well:

Active sprint view

And we can see, in its simplest form, we've got things that need to be done, we've got things that are in progress, and we've got things that have been completed.

Our **Quick filters** are also available for us here, so we can use them to refine the view. We might set up a quick filter for all of the different team members that are going to be working on stories in this sprint and put them across the top. Then, as we're going through a daily scrum, the scrum master might click on each name and look at just the items for that person, and try and figure out if there are any impediments.

If we move into the upper-right corner on this page, we will see three ellipses (**...**). Let's go into **Board settings** and take a look at this. We were in here previously, setting up a quick filter for our **Test Component**. Look under the **General** settings for our board, as shown in the following screenshot:

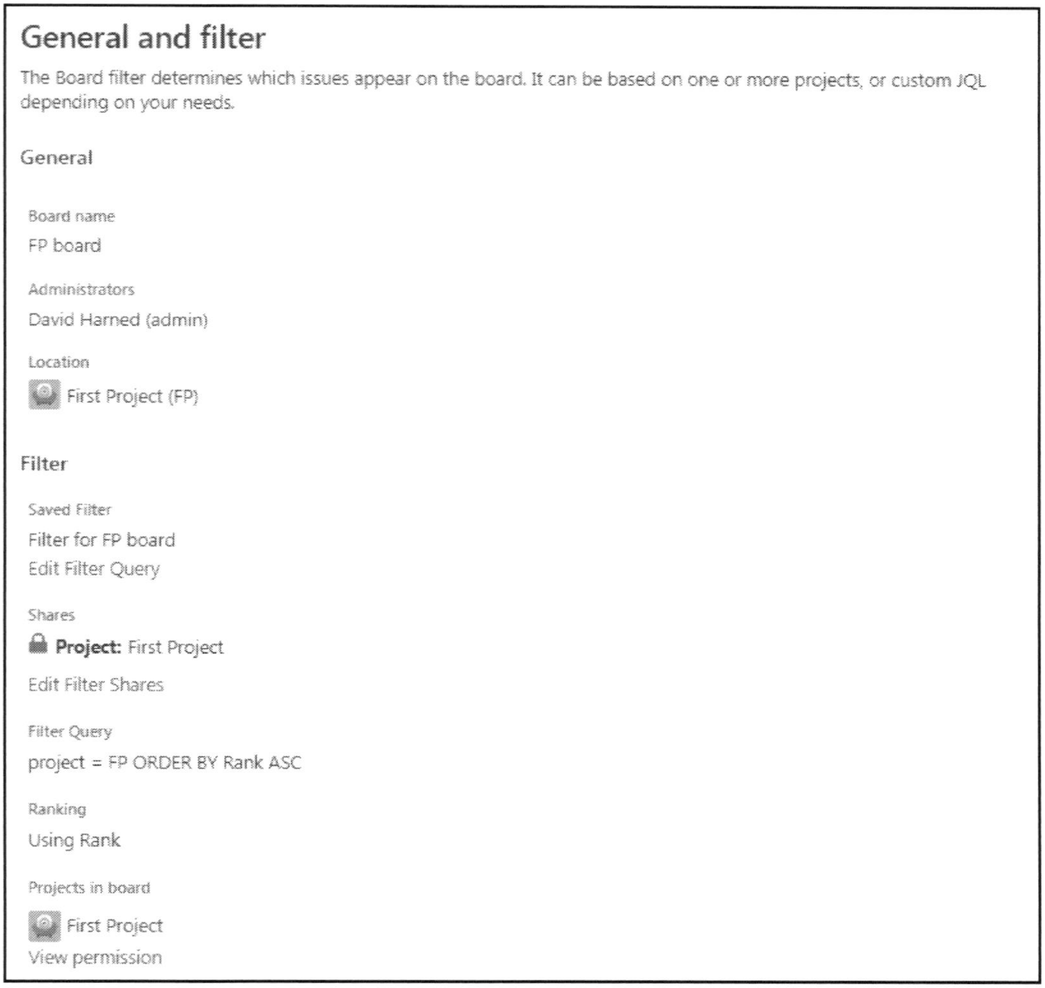

General and filter

The Board filter determines which issues appear on the board. It can be based on one or more projects, or custom JQL depending on your needs.

General

Board name
FP board

Administrators
David Harned (admin)

Location
🔘 First Project (FP)

Filter

Saved Filter
Filter for FP board
Edit Filter Query

Shares
🔒 **Project:** First Project

Edit Filter Shares

Filter Query
project = FP ORDER BY Rank ASC

Ranking
Using Rank

Projects in board
🔘 First Project
View permission

General board settings

We can see that we have things such as our **Board name**, which we can change regarding whether it appears here; the **Administrators**; and the **Location**. We can actually create queries and generate boards from our queries, but we're just using the JIRA default for this project. We can see that, in the preceding screenshot, we have the project, we have the query, and we can see that we've actually got multiple projects that we can put into a board as well, but we're going to leave these settings as they are.

Let's take a look at **Columns**:

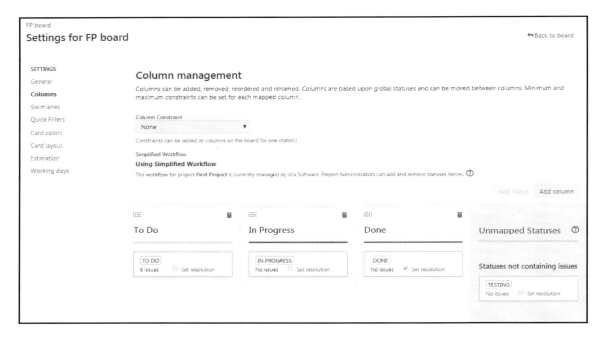

Managing columns on the FP board

We need to add a testing step to the workflow. When work items move from **TO DO** and then to **IN PROGRESS**, that is pretty clear. However, once they've been worked on, they need to be tested or validated before they're considered **DONE**. This way, we can maintain a high level of quality in what we are delivering. We have lots of testers in our scrum team, and this is going to work out just fine, because we can actually move a card into that testing column and we can have one of the testers help us with testing that.

We'll want to add a testing step to the workflow. To add that new column, we'll need another status to map it to. Do you remember that we created the **CLOSED** status in the workflow we managed in the previous section? We'll do the same thing now. I've created a **TESTING** status in my workflow, which you can see in the following screenshot:

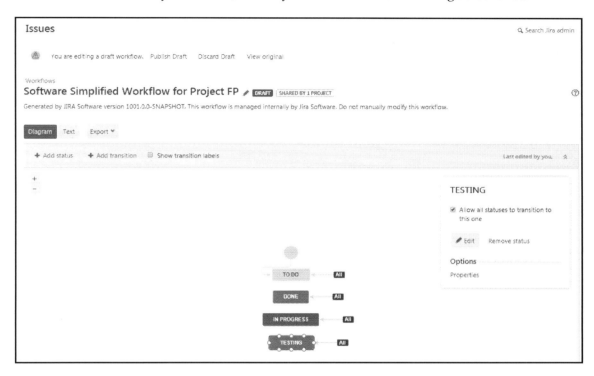

Adding a testing step to our workflow

What we've done is created a **TESTING** step. Any step can transition into this step. Now that we have this all set, let's go ahead and go back to our **First Project**. If we go back into **Active sprints** and then to our **Board settings**, then **Columns**, we can now add a column called Testing after the **In Progress** column. We can see that this column won't show on the board without a status, but that's okay because we created that status in the workflow. We can now move that status into the column we just created:

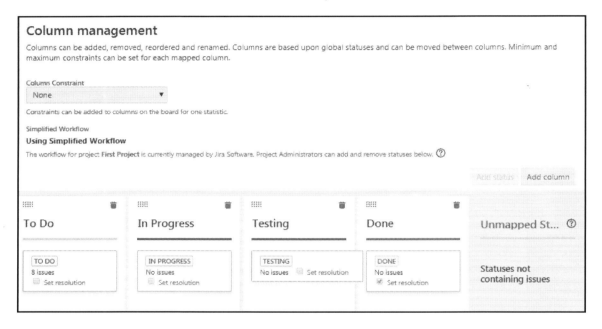

Column management

Great! Now, we have the **To Do**, **In Progress**, **Testing**, and **Done** columns. If we go back to the board, we'll see that we have a **Testing** column.

Next, we will take a look at **Swimlanes.**

Swimlanes actually cut across a board through all columns, and we can use them in a variety of different ways. JIRA gives us some options to do so:

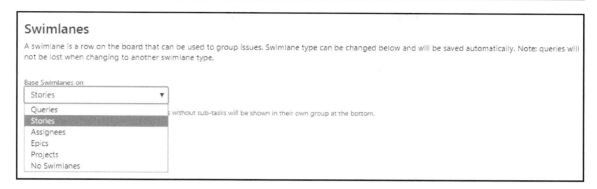

Swimlanes

By default, JIRA chooses **Stories**, but we could create a swimlane that you could expand or collapse for **Assignees** or **Epics.** Normally, if we've got stories with subtasks underneath them in our sprint, then our subtask will be what is shown on the board, and we can expand and collapse the stories as **Swimlanes**. We'll leave it at **Stories** for now.

We've already talked about **Quick filters**, so we can skip that one.

We've got some capabilities so that we can modify **Card colors** based on the options shown in the following screenshot:

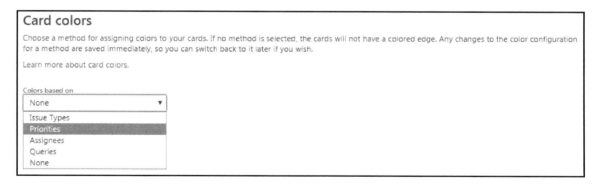

Card colors

In other words, if we've got a high-priority card, because the priority is set to high/critical, we can have it change color. We can also change the items that appear on our card, and we can show up to three additional fields in the **Card layout**. This allows us to pick what those three additional fields might be, but for now, we'll leave them as their default settings:

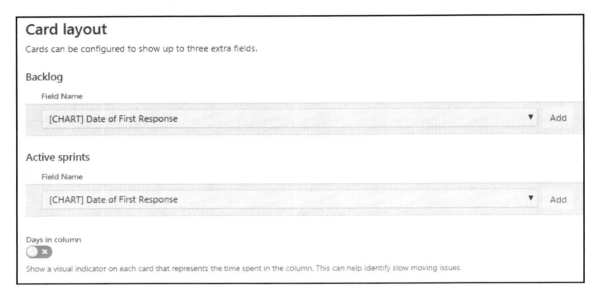

Card layout

Then, we've got **Estimation**. Generally, in scrum, we measure the velocity of our team in story points. We shouldn't really use time, as relative estimation is much more effective than time estimation. However, that is another book for another time. Lots of teams still use time to perform estimations, and this is how you would do it:

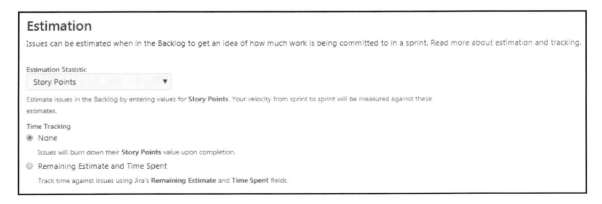

If we do use time and we're burning down hours, this would be where we would want to make that change. We would want a **Remaining Estimate and Time Spent**, we'd select the item, and then we would perform our estimation on the original time estimate.

Finally, **Working Days**, as we might imagine, is really about setting the working days for the group that's going to be using this board:

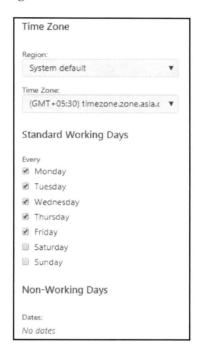

Configuring Working Days

We've configured all of this—we've got our board ready to go, and we've got our sprints with items in them. I think we're probably about ready to start a sprint, and that's what's going to happen in the next chapter.

Summary

Let's talk about what we learned in this chapter. We talked about what epics, stories, bugs, and tasks are, how to use each of them, and why we use one versus the other. We learned about the different work item attributes that are available to us, then learned what they are, and how to add or remove them so that we can configure JIRA to meet the needs of our team. Then, we learned how to manage the items that are in our backlog using prioritization, assigning to epics and versions, and more. Finally, we talked about what a board is, how to configure that board so that the workflow matches our workflow, and how to effectively manage those items as they go through a sprint.

In the next chapter, we're going to go ahead and start our first sprint.

Running Your Project in JIRA 3

In Chapter 1, *Get Started with Creating Projects*, we described JIRA, along with how to get started on creating projects in it. In Chapter 2, *Managing Work Items*, we discussed managing all of the different work items and their attributes in detail.

In this chapter, you'll learn about running your project, and how you can use JIRA to manage that.

In this chapter, we will cover the following topics:

- Creating and starting a sprint
- The daily scrum
- Smaller stories and tasks
- Closing the sprint – the sprint report

Creating and starting a sprint

In this section, we will cover the following topics:

- The backlog view, which allows us to prioritize the stories, tasks, bugs, and the elements within them
- Filtered views of the backlog
- Creating sprints to use as containers for the work
- Story point estimation
- Sizing the team commitment
- Adjustment to a sprint

Let's go to JIRA, and then to our **FP** project. This is the **Backlog** view, and we have some stories in the backlog, as shown in the following screenshot:

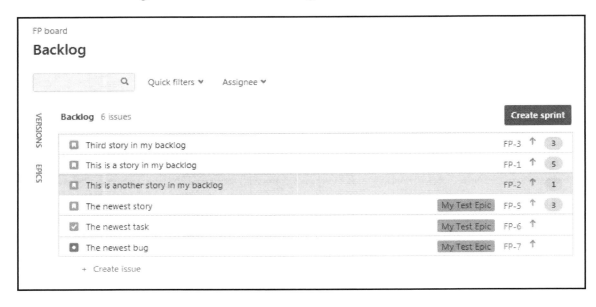

Backlog view

In the preceding screenshot, you can see four stories, a task, and a bug. We can prioritize these items by dragging and dropping them, and we can move them around and put them into whatever priority order we would like. The most important item will be on the top.

As shown in the preceding screenshot, these stories have point values. On the right-hand side of our first story, in the grey oval, we can see a story point value of 3; the one below it has a story point value of 1, and so on. Remember that these story points refer to the doubt, effort, and complexity contained within the items. We have the ability to edit these values by selecting an item and then going into the preview pane on the right, as follows:

Preview pane of FP1-24

We can edit some of these values, whether it's the **Status**, **Assignee**, **Labels**, **Story points**, and more; we also have the ability to filter by **Assignee**, as well as some other **Quick filters**, which include **Only My Issues**, **Recently Updated**, and more, in the drop-down menu. In the following screenshot, there's only one **Assignee**. In a real-life scenario, we would have our whole team listed:

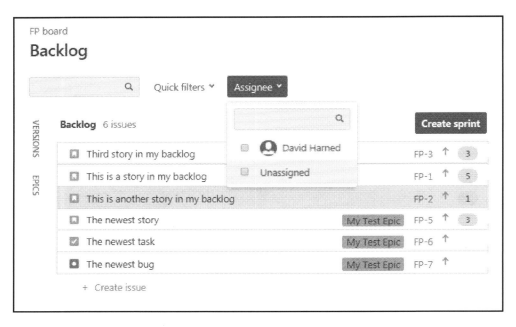

Assignee filter in the Backlog view

Now, we have a backlog with some items in it. Let's create a `Ready` sprint. Remember the *definition of ready* that we mentioned previously, which all of our items that have been fully refined should meet. It is important that we have enough detail to understand when the product owner thinks the item is done. Ideally, we want to have at least two sprints of ready work that are always available to the team.

Let's do that first. We'll create a sprint of work that is fully refined and meets the definition of ready. By clicking on the ellipses, we can edit the sprint and name it `Ready`, and we can include the **Sprint goal** as `Work that is fully refined`, as follows:

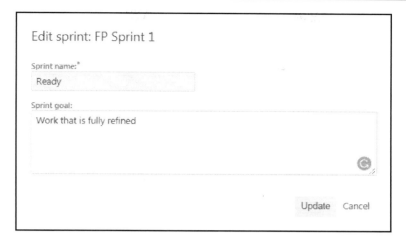

Rename the sprint Ready to fill with refined work

Now, we have a **Ready** sprint. We can see that the first three stories in our backlog look like they're ready to go. So, let's drag them up into that sprint:

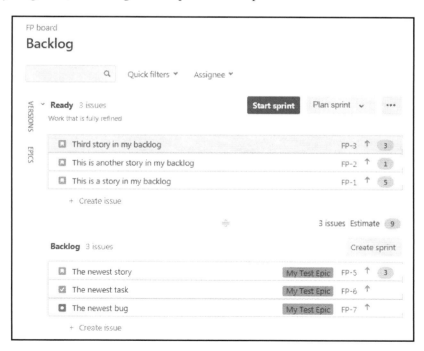

Next, let's create a sprint that we're actually going to execute.

We'll call this one FP1 Sprint 1, and we'll include This is my first Sprint as the **Sprint goal**:

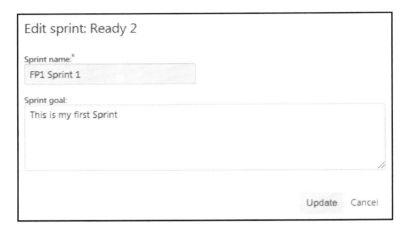

We can now take this sprint and drag it up above the **Ready** sprint, as shown in the following screenshot. Then, there is **Backlog** below them both that represents anything else that is in this list of things that we might want to eventually do:

We will now take two of the stories from the **Ready** sprint and drag them up into our sprint, as follows:

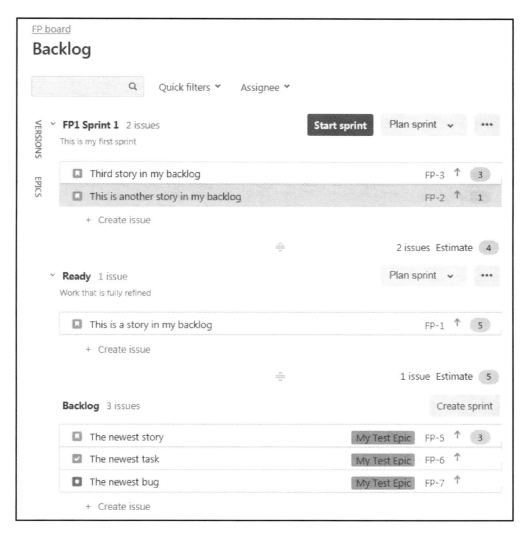

Moving work items from the Ready sprint into FP1 sprint 1

Now, you might be wondering, how do we know when we have enough story points loaded into our sprint? How do we know when we have enough work in there? These are great question to ask.

Until we have data to rely on, we want to try to get a group commitment on our first sprint. In our second sprint, we'll sort of do the same thing, based on the output of our first sprint. The number of story points that we complete in our sprint is called our **velocity**. We use the velocity from our previous sprint to help determine the velocity of the next sprint. We're able to complete it, and then adjust it accordingly. After three sprints, we'll have what's called **yesterday's weather**; the reason that they call it that is because yesterday's weather is known. We know what the weather was yesterday, but the weather for tomorrow is a forecast, and that's the best that we can do. It's usually pretty close, but it may not be exactly right. We can use yesterday's weather to create a commitment, which becomes the maximum that we'll want to plan to. You'll learn a little more about that when we look at velocity reports in a later chapter.

Given that as a team, **FP Sprint 1** doesn't have a previous velocity, we're going to go ahead and commit to four story points; we'll see whether or not we're able to complete them.

We have our sprint all ready to go; the story points are there, all of the stories meet our *definition of ready*, and we even have some additional stuff to do, in case we finish these things early. Let's go ahead and start our sprint, as follows:

You'll see that we have the ability to name the sprint (which we've done already); we can set the duration of this sprint and its start and end dates, and we can define the sprint's goal. Let's go ahead and look at the following screen:

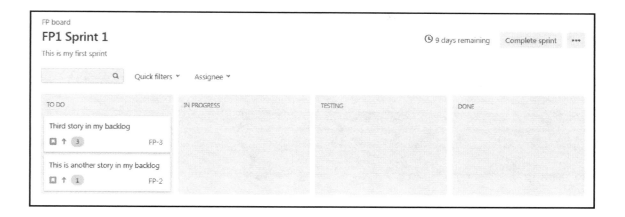

The daily scrum

Now, we have a sprint running. In this section, we'll discuss the daily scrum.

In this section, you'll learn about the following topics:

- How to use JIRA daily, as we're moving through a sprint
- How to use the board and burndown points or hours
- How to know whether sprint is on or off track

During a sprint, we want to use JIRA to move sprint work items through a workflow. We have our board with the columns on it—**To Do**, **In Progress**, and **Done**. We want to use JIRA to make sure that we're on track, because if we're doing a two-week sprint, we want to know as soon as possible whether we're on track, so that we can make adjustments in real time. We need to be able to generate data that we're going to need for reports at the end of the sprint, and JIRA will do that for us automatically. We just need to follow some day-to-day process stuff. Let's facilitate the daily scrum ceremony by using JIRA.

Let's hop back over to JIRA. As you'll remember from the previous section, we created a sprint called **FP Sprint 1**, we had our queue of ready work, and we had the rest of the backlog. However, since that sprint has just started, let's take a look at a sprint that's already running. Let's move over to our **Second Project**.

As you can see in the following screenshot, we are in the middle of **SP Sprint 1**. We can see the items that are contained within the sprint. There's the **Ready** sprint of items that are ready to go, and then, there are a couple of stories that are in the **Backlog**, in order of priority:

While we are in a sprint, we will want to look at the **Active sprints** view, which shows us the Scrum board:

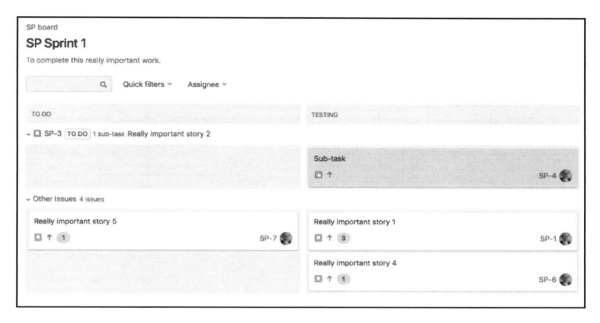

Active sprints view

Suppose that we're meeting in our daily scrum, and that we've brought our team together for 15 minutes. Let's take a look at our burndown and get a sense of whether we are on or off track for this Now, we need to go around the room and ask people three questions, as follows:

- What impediments are keeping us from meeting our sprint commitment?
- Are we doing anything that will prevent our squad or other teams from meeting their sprint commitments?
- Are there any new dependencies to discover, or any ways to resolve dependencies that we have discovered since our last daily scrum?

These are the three questions that we'll want to discuss with the team. As everyone is talking about the answers to those questions, and what impediments they are running into that will keep them from meeting their sprint commitments, we'll be updating the board in real time. They can also do this prior to the meeting, of course.

Let's take a look at the preceding screenshot. We have a story, the **SP-3** story, which we can expand or collapse (remember **Swimlanes**?). We also have a **Sub-task** that exists underneath it. We might have stories with sub-tasks, and we might also have stories without sub-tasks. JIRA will display the smallest increment of work as the item to move on the board. Beneath that, we can see our other issues, and these other issues are all story-level items, without sub-tasks underneath them. We can see that story number 3, or **SP-5**, has already been completed, and has been moved to **Done**. Because of that, we're going to move the **Sub-task** over to the **DONE** column; you'll see that when we do that, JIRA will actually prompt us with the following message. We can say yes by clicking on the **Update** button:

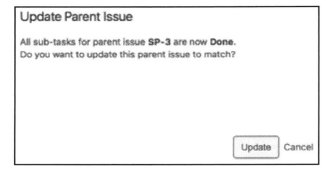

SP-3 is now complete, along with the sub-tasks underneath it. We'll move **SP-7** to **Testing**, because we have already completed development, and it needs to be validated:

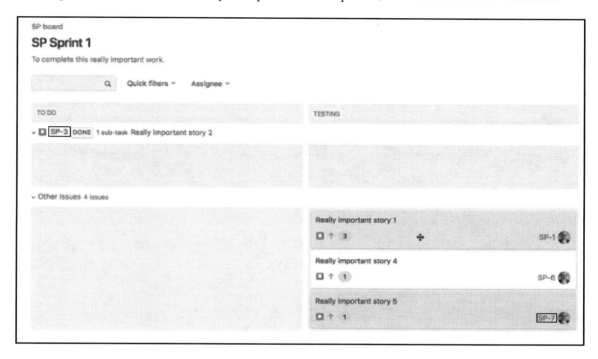

Moving JIRA the SP-7 item to the TESTING column

Let's take a look at our burndown and get a sense of whether we are on or off track for this sprint. We'll go to **Reports** and look at the **Burndown Chart**. Let's take a look at how to read this **Burndown Chart**, as follows:

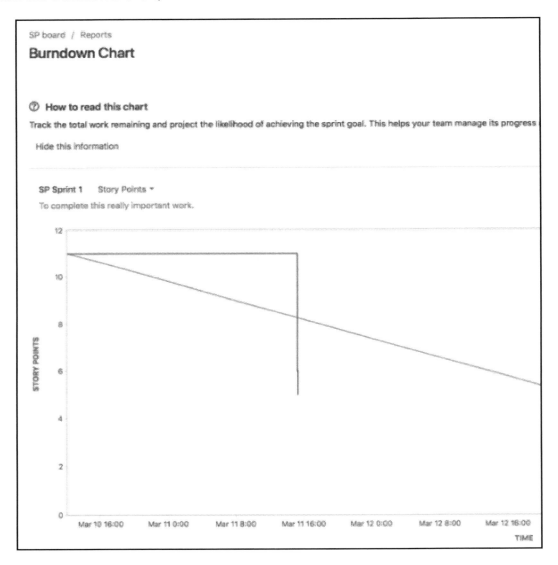

Screenshot showing the Burndown Chart

On the left-hand side, we have **STORY POINTS**, and on the bottom, we have **TIME**. What this shows us is that at the beginning of the sprint, we had a certain amount of story points of work to do. Every time that we move one of these work items to the **DONE** column, that story's story points are decremented from the overall story points. We can see that the gray line in the preceding screenshot represents the ideal.

At the beginning of the sprint, we had 11 story points, and at the end of the sprint, we will have zero story points, because they'll all be done. What this burndown tells us is that for **SP-1**, when we're looking at the story points in **SP Sprint 1**, we're actually ahead of schedule. We can see that we have a burndown of some story points, but five still remain for the sprint; even so, we're actually ahead of the ideal line. We'll want to walk through this with our team. We'll review the **Burndown Chart** together and say—*Hey team, looks like we're doing really well; we're ahead of schedule. There's a pretty good chance we're going to finish these items, in which case, we'll want to be pulling them from the ready queue and adding more work.*

That's how we run a daily scrum in JIRA.

Smaller stories and tasks

In this section, we'll discuss whether we should have smaller stories or tasks, and how we should organize our work in the most effective way for our team.

In the previous sections, we set up our sprint and started it, and we looked at how we can use JIRA within a daily Scrum. Now, we'll discuss the work itself. What is the best way for the work to be structured in JIRA? Should we have one story per person? Should we use sub-tasks under a story to make things more specific?

The answers depend on different factors, which is one of the things that makes this so challenging. It depends on the team; it depends on how we work; and there are some key things that we need to be thinking about as we're structuring our work. Really, it's about speed. It's about delivering the most work in the amount of time that a sprint iteration is. Discussing the fastest teams, and thinking about the concepts that help teams become faster, can help us to focus on the goals of the team, and not the individual. That's one of the things that's really challenging.

We can structure our work in a way that has a story per person, but really, it's about making sure that the team is operating optimally as a team, not as a group of individuals. **Swarming** is a team concept that brings speed. Having the UX, development, backend development, and testers all attacking one story and moving through that one story, and then attacking the next story, is really the quickest way for the team to work, as opposed to each person working on their own thing. It helps to improve performance so that we can keep commitments realistic and get it all done.

Previously, we discussed using yesterday's weather as a barometer for how much work to commit to in a sprint. We could commit to more than that, and maybe we would complete it, but it's really about team motivation. If we commit to 10 points and we complete 12, that makes the team feel happy; if we commit to 15 and complete 12, the team feels like they didn't do a good job, and this will actually demotivate them, even if they deliver the same 12 points. We want to make sure that the team is motivated and excited about what they're doing. If we can keep the commitment realistic, it will allow the team to commit and finish the work that they committed to, and then, they can pull more from that ready queue that we created. This is really important if they're going to be delivering more than 100 percent of their commitment consistently. It will also cause the average velocity of the team to increase over time, which is a good thing.

Now, let's look at relative sizing, instead of specific sizing. If people commit to working through a story for eight hours, and then it takes ten hours, they will struggle with meeting their commitment. It is highly unlikely that someone will estimate the exact right time for the work that they need to do. Using relative sizing allows us to instead focus on the team commitment. If a story has three points, then we'll be able to relatively size that against the other stories in the sprint, so that a three-point story in one sprint is the same as a three-point story in the last sprint. We don't need to know whether that item is six and a half hours or eight and a half hours; we know that it's a three.

The last concept that you should be considering in your team is having **T-shaped people**. This means imagining a person with their arms outstretched to either side, so that they look like a **T**. They're deep in a skill set in the middle of that T, and their arms represent two other skills that they might also have. The more that we do to make our team cross-functional, the more we can increase the throughput of the team. Maybe that tester is also pretty good at process, so they can help to serve as the Scrum Master. Maybe we have a UX designer who can also do some frontend coding. This will allow us to actually increase the speed of the project when people swarm on a story, letting everyone do as much as they can. It will help us to utilize all of the team's capacity.

Let's take a look at JIRA, and how JIRA supports these ideas. We'll walk through a couple of these concepts. Moving back to our **Backlog**, what's important to remember is that we discussed the fact that a board shows the smallest unit of work.

If we have a story in our backlog, the team needs to work on that story. However, we might want to get more specific, if we have multiple people contributing to the story in order to get it done. We can create a task for UX, create a task for frontend development, and create a task for backend development. We will have a person that is accountable for the story overall, and then, we can create sub-tasks for each of the activities within the story, which will allow us to capture each one of those work streams underneath. Again, remember that it's not about what's best for the individual; it's about what's best for the story, and for the team overall.

We already discussed that when we move a story into **Done**, we decrement those five story points from the Sprint, but if we want to track this in regard to hours, we can do that, too. When we select any item in the **Backlog** or **Board** view, we have a preview pane; under **show more**, we can actually do time tracking, as well.

It's important to note that we can do this, as some teams prefer to work in increments of time:

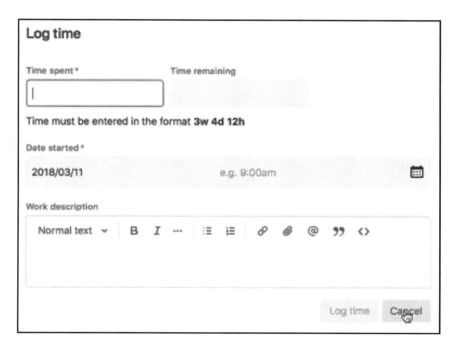

Tracking time during a sprint in JIRA

If we do, then we can look at the time spent and the time remaining, and we can actually burn hours instead of story points in our burndown. On the left-hand side, where we would have story points, we will instead have hours. If these were the number of hours that were required in order to finish our commitment, then the hours would burn to zero, which means that as we finished our stories, we would want to update the time spent and the time remaining.

Hopefully, these tips will help us to figure out what's best for our team. Go ahead and experiment; this should be the way that we choose to handle our items in JIRA.

Closing the sprint – the sprint report

In this section, we'll cover closing our sprint. In the previous sections, we discussed creating and starting the sprint, how to use JIRA to run our daily Scrum, and how we should configure our work (whether we should use smaller stories or tasks). We try to figure out what's most useful to the team. In this section, we will discuss closing and completing the sprint.

Let's take a look at JIRA. We were working on **SP Sprint 1**. We've finished the really important stories (numbers **1**, **3**, **4**, and **6**), as shown in the following screenshot. We can see that these are all done. However, story number **5** (**SP-7**) is not done. For the sake of our demo, we can still go ahead and complete our sprint, anyway:

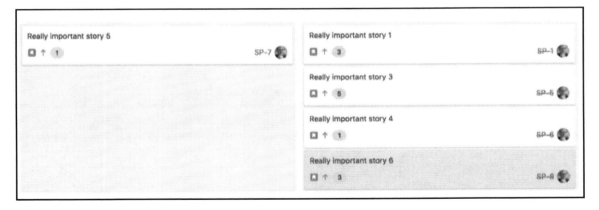

Not all of the work is in the DONE column

We're going to hit the **Complete** button; in the following screenshot, you can see that five issues were completed, and one issue was incomplete. It prompts me by saying—Where do you want to put that incomplete issue? Do you want to put it in the **Backlog**, or do you want to put it in the **Ready** (next) sprint? We'll go ahead and put it back into the **Ready** sprint, then we'll complete our sprint:

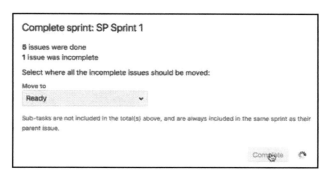

Prompt regarding next steps for incomplete work items

The following screenshot shows a **Sprint Report** for this sprint:

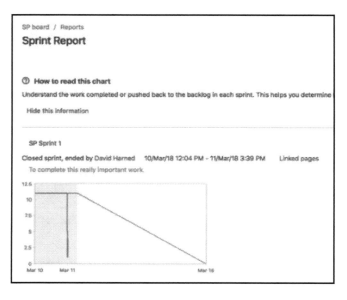

Sprint Report

There are a few things to look at. First of all, we discussed the burndown, and in the preceding screenshot, we can see that we originally started with 11 story points, and we were able to burn down to one. We completed 10 story points in this sprint. We can see the completed issues, and we can also see the items, the number of those items, and the amount of story points that were done.

Then, there's **SP-8**, which is story 6, as shown in the following screenshot. We added it after the sprint had started. We can see the issue that was added to the sprint after its start time, because it has an asterisk by the ID:

Completed Issues		
Key	Summary	Issue Type
SP-1	Really important story 1	▢ Story
SP-3	Really important story 2	▢ Story
SP-5	Really important story 3	▢ Story
SP-6	Really important story 4	▢ Story
SP-8 *	Really important story 6	▢ Story

Completed work items within the sprint

We did not complete issue 7, **SP-7**, which was story 5 and was really important, so that was one story point that we didn't get, and that is also shown here:

Issues Not Completed		
Key	Summary	Issue Type
SP-7	Really important story 5	▢ Story

Incomplete work items within the sprint

The good news is that we were able to complete 13 story points for our 11-point commitment. The bad news, of course, is that we didn't finish one story point, and that story was more important than the one that we added. We did complete 13 with 11 as our commitment, so we delivered our commitment, plus a little more. Hopefully, not completing this one story was okay for our product owner, and they will still approve this sprint.

Summary

In this chapter, we learned how to use JIRA to run our project, how to create a sprint, and how to bring refined backlog items in so that we can have a sprint that meets the definition of ready. We determined how big a sprint commitment should be, using yesterday's weather to help us. You also learned how to start a sprint, and how to use JIRA during a daily Scrum and throughout the sprint. We looked at burndowns and board views.

We also discussed how to best help the sprint succeed by using JIRA as a tool, and the different concepts used to structure work, so that our team is most effective as they're moving through the sprint in the board view, either through sub-tasks or smaller stories. Finally, you learned how to complete a sprint.

In the next chapter, we'll discuss reporting.

4
Working with Reports

In this chapter, you'll learn about versions and releases—what they are, and how they're different from each other. We'll discuss how to read burndowns, sprint reports, and velocity charts in order to determine whether your team is doing well. We will take a look at release and epic burndowns, as well as version and epic reports, which will give us the ability to do forecasting, a very powerful tool.

This chapter will cover the following topics:

- Versions and releases
- Burndown reports
- Sprint reports
- Velocity charts
- Release and epic burndowns
- Version and epic reports

Versions and releases

Let's start with versions and releases. In this section, you'll learn what versions and releases are, and how they interact with one another. We'll discuss how to create and manage versions, how to assign work to versions, how to perform a release, and finally, how to view the contents of a release once we've created it.

Versions come from the concept of software. We're all familiar with the major and minor versions of a software (for example, version 2.0 versus version 2.1). These represent a large amount of value, so that's a way to think about it—a version represents a chunk of value that's being deployed. Versions can be released, so once we've determined what's in a version and we've completed it, we can release it, and that version will become a release. They're the same thing, but one is pre-deployment, and one is post-deployment. Once a version has been released, we can view the contents of that version as release notes, so we'll take a look at that, too.

Let's hop over to JIRA and take a look at our **Second Project**. In the **Backlog**, we can see that we have **VERSIONS**. We can actually take a look at these versions by clicking on them:

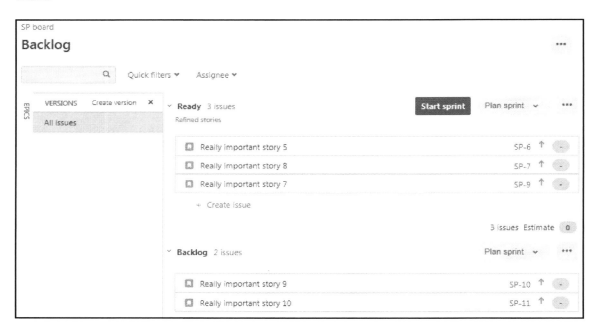

Expanding the Versions Pane in the Backlog view

As you can see in the preceding screenshot, this is where all of our versions will be available to map work items to. We mentioned previously that a version is essentially a release, before it's been released. They are the same thing. So, let's go under **Releases** in the left-hand column menu, and click on the **Create version** button. You'll see the following screenshot:

Prompt to Create a Version

In the preceding screenshot, you can see the version **Name**, a **Start Date**, the **Release date**, and a **Description**. Let's make a version and call it `test version`. The **Start Date** and **Release date** are optional, but let's go ahead and write `test version` in the **Description**. Then, we'll click on **Save**:

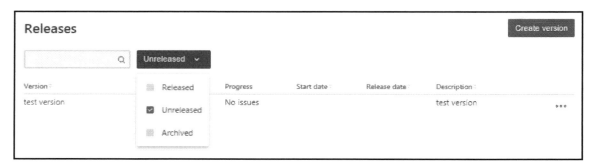

Filtering the Versions in our project

On the **Releases** page, we have the option to look at **Released**, **Unreleased**, and **Archived** versions. We also have our test version. We can create another one if we want to. In the following screenshot, within the line item, we have the ability to **Release**, **Archive**, and more:

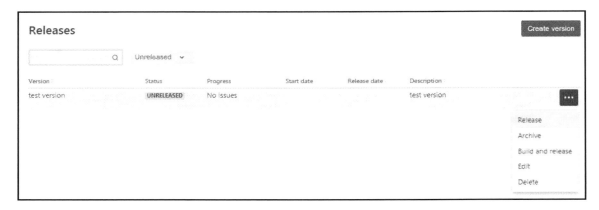

Options we have for Versions

If we go back to our **Backlog** and click on the **VERSIONS** tab on the left-hand side, as shown in the following screenshot, we will see the test version that we created. We can see **Issues**, **Completed**, **Unestimated**, and more:

Viewing Versions in the Backlog view

Now, we can take two stories and drag them on top of the version in the interface. If we do that, as shown in the following screenshot, these stories will now be a part of the test version:

Adding work items to a Version in the Backlog view

If we go under **Releases** again, we can take a look at the version. In the following screenshot, there are two issues in this version (the two that we added), and there are no issues done, none in progress, and two in to do:

Viewing the contents of a Version

Now, go back to the **Backlog,** and we'll put another three stories into this **VERSION**. This means that we will now have five issues within. We'll go back to **Releases**, and then we'll go ahead and release our version by clicking the button in the top-right corner.

We've now released the version. If we click on the link to go to our **Release notes**, we will see what was contained within our version, and we can even cut and paste the HTML, if we need that format:

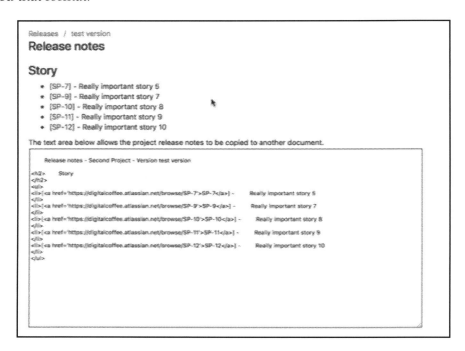

Test version's release notes

Burndown reports

Now, we'll discuss burndown reports. You may have seen a burndown before, but now, you'll learn how to use it during a sprint iteration in Scrum. In this section, we're going to discuss the report (as used in JIRA) more specifically, including how we read it and what kinds of data we can use from it.

As you already know, a burndown is used to measure the progress within an iteration, and it helps us to understand whether we are on or off track from our ideal state as we go along. In a burndown, the vertical axis represents the total amount of work that exists inside of that iteration, and the horizontal axis represents the time.

Burndowns tell us stories. The more we look at them, the more we will understand what may or may not have happened during an iteration; we get pretty good at telling the story by looking at the burndowns. If we start to get creative, we can also burn down all kinds of things: points, hours, risks, and more.

Burndown example one

Now, we'll take a look at how to view burndowns in JIRA. Let's look at the following example:

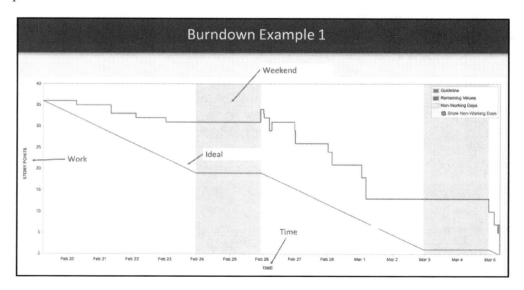

Burndown example 1

First of all, on the vertical axis, we have **STORY POINTS**. In this iteration, we have about 36 story points at the beginning of the sprint. At the end, we actually want to burn down to zero story points, so ideally, we're handling all of the work that was committed to in this iteration. On the bottom, we have **TIME**. This would be a two-week sprint, and we can see that as we go through time, we burn down the story points to zero, and no work will remain. The gray line represents the ideal scenario; so, assuming that the work is being moved through correctly, we want to be close to that gray line. This would show the pattern that we're looking for. The gray vertical bars represent a weekend, or a time that the team is not working; they're flat, because ideally, we're not working on the weekends. We can also see that there's a blue checkbox in the upper-right that says **Show Non-Working Days**. We can uncheck that and get rid of those weekends if we don't want to look at them.

Burndown example two

Burndowns can tell us a story about the sprint. Let's take a look at the following burndown example:

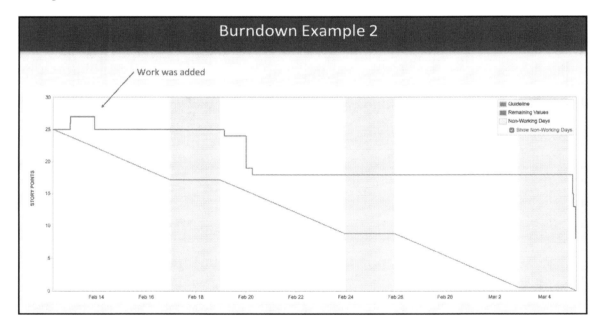

Burndown example 2

One of the things that we want to keep an eye on, as we can see at the beginning of this particular three-week sprint, is that we started with 25 story points, and at the end of the sprint, we didn't quite burn down to zero. There's a little hump in red; this hump is caused by work being added to the sprint once it was already started. It also looks like not much was done in the last two weeks, as no story points were burned, and a lot of the points got finished right at the end of the sprint. These would be great topics for the team's retrospective.

Burndown report

Let's take a look at the JIRA reports by clicking on the **Reports** link in the left-hand column. The burndown chart is the first item that we'll see, and that is how we can get to our burndown:

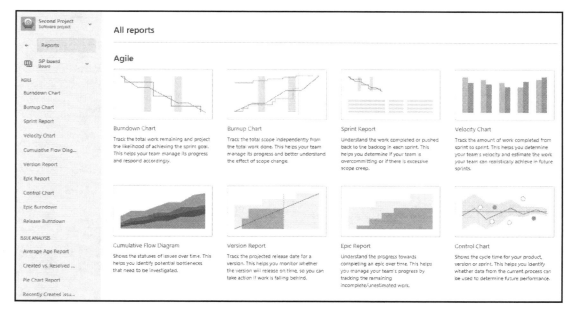

Many reports are available within JIRA

Let's talk about burning down other values. If we go back to our **Backlog**, in the upper-right corner, within our **Board** settings, we'll see **Estimation**:

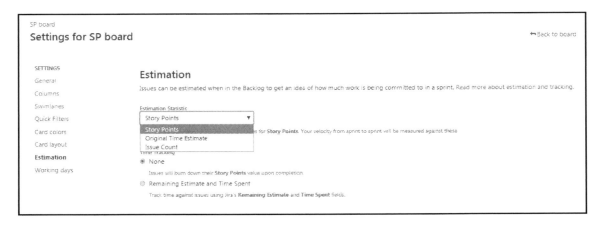

Estimates in Story Points or other values

In the preceding screenshot, we're estimating in story points, but we also have the **Original Time Estimate** as an option. If we select this, we can use time tracking, so that instead of seeing story points on the vertical axis, we'll actually see hours in our burndown. Supposing that we have an item that started with 10 hours, we can update the value to be, say, eight hours or six hours long, and it will actually burn down the amount of hours, instead of the story points, as we move through the sprint.

Sprint reports

In this section, we'll discuss the sprint report. We'll cover what it is, and we'll show how to read it. In the sprint report, there's a summary of the sprint iteration. It shows us the burndown, the work that was completed, the work that wasn't completed, and any work that was added and removed during the iteration.

Let's take a look at JIRA and get more information about a **Sprint Report**. You will need to have completed a sprint to have this data. We did run a one-day sprint in the SP project, so we have something to look at. First, click on **Reports** (on the left), and take a look at our **Sprint Report**:

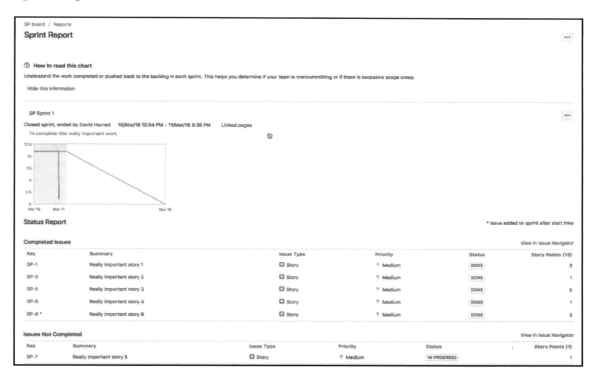

View of the Sprint Report

Keep in mind that our burndown is not going to be beautiful, because this was a one-day sprint. Normally, the burndown would be more appropriate, based on the iteration length of our sprint. Let's pay closer attention to the bottom of the report. As we can see in the preceding screenshot, we have the **Completed Issues**. If you see any issues that were added after the sprint started, you'll notice that they have an asterisk by them, which allows you to identify items that came in, but which were not a part of the original commitment. **SP-8** is an example of work that was added after the sprint was started. We can also see items that were not completed; **SP-7** was not completed during this sprint. We can also see any items that were removed from the sprint. In total, we have completed items, added items, removed items, and anything that was not completed. Of course, we also have the sprint name, and the date range for that sprint, as well.

Velocity charts

In this section, we'll discuss velocity charts. Velocity charts are very valuable. We'll cover what they are, how to read them, and how to use our past velocity to plan our future commitments.

Velocity charts – an example

Let's take a look at an example of a velocity chart, as follows:

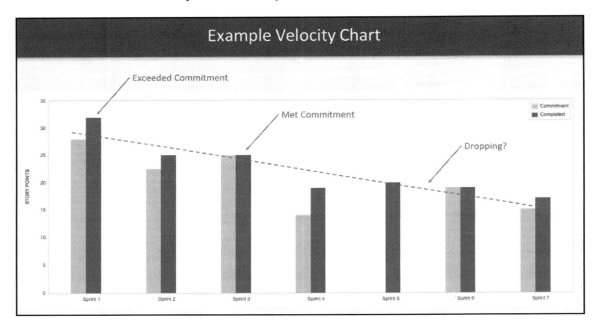

Velocity chart example

To orient us to the preceding chart, let's take a look at its different elements. The gray bars represent what we've committed to in each of our sprints, and we can see that this is measured in **STORY POINTS**. In this example, we can see that in **Sprint 3**, we've actually committed to **25** story points. The green bar represents what the team finished, and in this example, we've completed **25** story points, and we've met 100 percent of our commitment. That's great! We can also see some examples where the gray bar is lower than the green bar, which means that we actually completed even more than we committed to, which is even better!

If we look at **Sprint 5**, it doesn't have a commitment, so there may have been some sort of data problem there; or, there was no commitment, and the sprint was started without a commitment in place, which means that we would probably see a burn up when sprint work was added after the beginning of the iteration. We have already discussed how reports tell a story; this report tells a different story, which is interesting. We can see that our velocity is actually dropping, which could be a cause for alarm, and would be something to talk about with our Scrum Master (or with the team, if we're looking at this report). It's important to use these reports as a way to gather some knowledge and have transparency about what's going on with the project and team.

When planning a sprint commitment, the team should use the average velocity of the work completed in the last three sprints as their guide. Of course, they should have work ready to go at the top of the backlog, in case they can do more, but by using the past average velocity to create the commitment, it means that we are not just guessing. We have data that tells us how much work the team has completed historically, and that increases the likelihood of success for the team and takes the guesswork out. In addition, an attainable commitment means that the teams will meet their commitments. That makes the teams happy.

Release and epic burndowns

In this section, we'll discuss release and epic burndowns, how important they are, and how we can use them to give us some insight into how things are going. You're going to learn about what release and epic burndowns are, how to read the reports, and how to use the reports for forecasting.

Release burndown – an example

Now, we will look at an example of a release burndown.

Keep in mind that a release is a version. Essentially, it's a version that's been deployed. An epic is also a container of work, and is independent of a version.

Releases and epics are both containers for work. An epic is a large story that spans multiple sprints. Although a release is generally larger than an epic, the same concepts apply to both in regards to these reports; so, when we're looking at an epic burndown report, it's going to be the same as a release burndown report, but probably smaller, with fewer items and a shorter duration. However, it will allow us to predict when that specific epic might be completed.

Let's take a look at the following **Release Burndown** as an example. We want to familiarize ourselves with the different elements of this report:

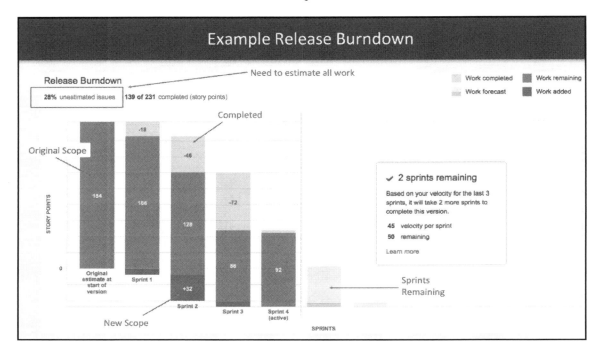

Release burndown example

First of all, in the first column, we're seeing an estimate of the work that's contained within this version, which will eventually be our release. We can see that it has **184** points. 28 percent of the issues that are contained within this version do not have story point estimates, which means that our original scope is actually larger than the **184**, but we don't have that work sized, which means that it would be very important to go and make sure that all of the work is sized so that it's all contained within our forecast right away. Until it is sized, it is essentially hidden. As we mentioned before, those **184** points represent our original scope, so the medium blue bar represents the original scope of the version at the time of creation. The dark blue in the preceding example (plus **32** points from **Sprint 2**) represents the new scope. This is work that was added in this iteration to this version, and is now a part of this release. The green portion of the bar represents work that's been completed; so, in **Sprint 2**, we finished **46** points of the original scope, and added **32** points. We still have **128** points of the original scope remaining. Given this, we can see that we have established a velocity. We know that this team's velocity is **45** points per sprint, and, based on that, we can see the dashed line and where we are today. We know that we have **50** story points remaining in the scope of this version. This tells us that we have just over a sprint's worth of work, so there are two sprints remain to get it done. If our two sprints are two weeks each, then we can forecast that there is one month remaining before this version will be available for release.

Version and epic reports

In this section about reporting, we'll discuss version and epic reports. In the previous section, we talked about release and epic burndowns, and we'll get a similar kind of view in this report, but a different look with slightly different information. In this section, you're going to learn what version and epic reports are.

Like the release and epic burndowns, a version report is large, containing a larger piece of value; an epic is smaller. These two are basically the same kind of report, but allow us to look at a specific version or a specific epic; then, we get some sort of a forecast as to when that item will be completed. We'll look at how to read a version report, and then we'll look at how we can use these reports to provide a forecast.

Version report – an example

An example of a version report is as follows:

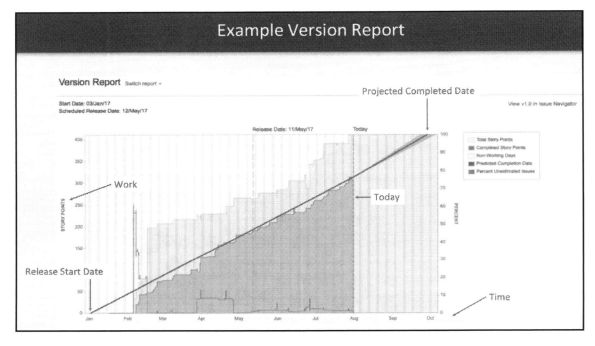

Example Version Report

In the preceding figure, we can see the work in the vertical axis, represented in **STORY POINTS**. We can see that there are actually quite a few story points in the preceding report, because usually, a version has a lot of value built into it. The horizontal axis represents **TIME**. There's a red line in the report that represents the amount of unestimated work as it goes up and down (as we move through this version). From the blue line, we can see that this version started in January; we can see **Today**, which is represented by a dotted line; and we can see that we have a projected completion date. Some other things to note are that the completed date is a cone shape, and that there's an optimistic date a little bit to the left of that projected completion date; a little bit to the right of that is a pessimistic date. One point of interest in this report is that the intended release date was May 11, which is in the (far) past. Hopefully, the release of your version is more on-time than this one. That needs to be adjusted.

The version report provides an optimistic and pessimistic release date, in addition to the projected date, based on the actual velocity of the team and the work that's included inside of that version. This value is actually dynamically generated as we move through time. If we remove the scope from this version, it will pull the date in and will deliver earlier; and, if the team slows down or if we add more scope, then that date will get pushed out. The closer we get to the projected completion date, the tighter that cone gets, until there's no more cone left at all. When we first started in February or March, we would have had a much wider cone, given the fact that there are a lot of variables that could affect that completion date. This gives us the useful ability to look at this version over time, and to figure out what that completion date might look like, and do some things very far ahead that would allow us to affect that. We have lots of choices, assuming that we have a good view of what lies ahead.

Summary

That brings us to the end of this chapter. In this chapter, you learned about versions and releases; what information release and epic burndown reports have, and how to read them; what a sprint report is; the data that's inside of a sprint report, and how to read it. You also saw what a velocity report looks like and why it's important for planning future sprints. We covered what version and epic reports are, and how to read them; we discussed the version and epic reports, and used them to provide forecasts for when a version will be completed.

In the next chapter, we'll discuss searching and filtering.

Issue Searching and Filtering

5

In this chapter, we'll discuss searching and filtering for issues, which is a very powerful capability within JIRA. We'll cover JQL, including what it is, how to write queries in JIRA using simple and advanced editors, and how to export your results.

In this chapter, we will cover the following topics:

- Issue searching using JQL
- Saving and managing filters
- Executing bulk changes
- Creating new boards from saved filters

Issue searching using JQL

In this section, we'll discuss issue searching using JQL. We will cover what JQL is, writing queries in both the simple editor and the advanced editor in order to return results, and how to export those results to use them in other ways.

First, let's talk about JQL. You won't want to confuse it with the Java Query Language, which is something different. We will be looking at the **JIRA Query Language** (**JQL**). It's very similar in format to SQL, so if you have spent any time with SQL and understand its query syntax, you're going to feel pretty comfortable in JQL. It uses fields, values, operators, and keywords. Let's discuss what those are.

The fields themselves are the different types of information that are contained within the systems; these are the different attributes for the work types, and more. The values are actually what's contained within those fields, so they are the actual values that we will be looking for. The operators are essentially the heart of the query—they're the intelligence—so they are things like equal to, not equal to, less than, and more than, which we can use to create some intelligence around the fields and values. Then, there are keywords, which are really reserved words that we use in our query language to connect these different operators together.

A post on the Atlassian website that covers searching JIRA more thoroughly can be seen at `https://confluence.atlassian.com/jiracore/blog/2015/07/search-jira-like-a-boss-with-jql`.

Simple and advanced JQL editors in JIRA

Let's take a look at the simple and advanced JQL editors in JIRA.

We have two projects, named **First Project** and **Second Project**, in our instance of JIRA. We want to run some queries against these projects. Go to the **Issues and filters** link in the left-hand column:

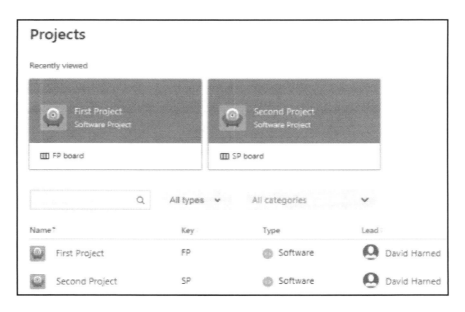

Dashboard containing projects

Our default screen for searching is basically the most generic query that we can do, and we're actually in the advanced editor. Let's flip over to the basic editor by clicking on the link in the upper right-hand corner of the screen:

Basic query editor is easy to use

As you can see in the preceding screenshot, the basic editor gives us drop-down menus that will allow us to build a query. Now, we can select the values for the attributes. Let's suppose that we only want to see the **First Project** or the **Second Project**; if we select those checkboxes, the items being returned in the search will change. We can also select the types of issues that we want to see, the statuses that we want to see, who the issue is assigned to, and more. In the basic editor, we can run a query by just clicking and searching for issues.

 If you get stuck, you can write some of your JQL query in the basic editor, and then switch to the advanced editor to see the actual JQL query text and modify it there. There are many good resources on the web for writing JQL, if you need help.

If we go to the advanced editor, there are (of course) more advanced possibilities. This simple query shows all of the work items, ordered by the date that they were created:

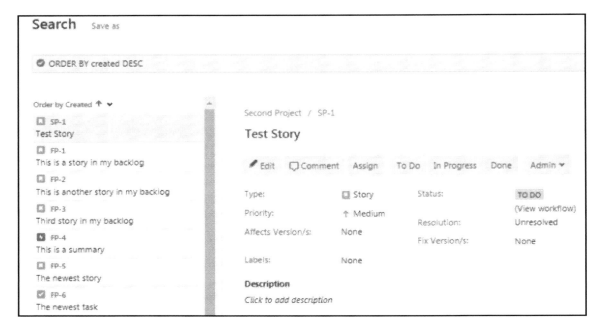

Advanced query editor brings more capability in JQL

Let's have some more fun. We can show all of the stories in open sprints within the **FP-1** project, and order them by the date that they were created, descending. We can search for work items that are of the type **Story** within the first project, which we can refer to by its **Key**, **FP-1**. Here is that query:

Query to return stories in open sprints within project FP1

We will get back two stories. These are the two stories that are currently in the **First Project**, and that are in an open sprint.

In this section, we looked at how we can write a query in both the basic and advanced query editor, and you were also given a nice little hint for how to search in open sprints.

Saving and managing filters

In this section, we'll discuss saving and managing filters. You're going to learn how to save a created filter, how to set permissions for saved filters, and how to see all of your saved filters, and then manage them.

Let's go back over to JIRA and take a look at our issue-searching screen. We have a query; so, let's flip over to the basic editor and say, show me everything that's in the second project. Saving this is really easy, as all you have to do is click on **Save as**, and this will take you to the following screen, where you should write `Second Project Work Items` as the **Filter Name**:

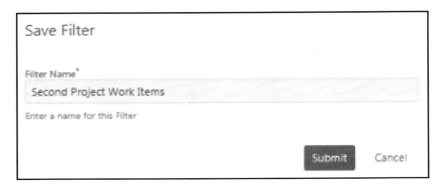

If we click on **Submit**, we will have a saved filter. We've taken a query and turned it into a filter by saving it, so that we can run it again and again. If we look under **Manage filters** on the left-hand side, we can see the filter that we just saved, called **Second Project Work Items**:

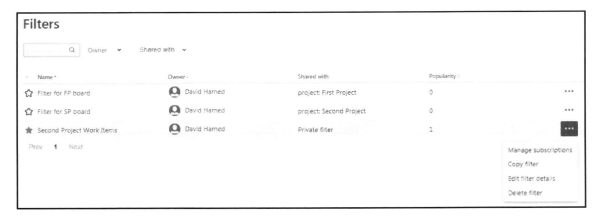

Filters for our project

We also have three ellipses on the right-hand side, which provide us with some options, such as **Manage subscriptions**, **Copy filter**, and **Edit filter details**; we can even click on **Shared with** and take a look at who these are shared with. If we click on the **Second Project** work items, we'll see the contents of that query. We can also click on **Advanced**, so that we can see the detailed text of the query that we used:

Second Project Work Items

In the top corner of the preceding screenshot, we can see that we can share the item by providing the link and inserting the username or email of the person contained within JIRA; then, we can add a **Note** and hit **Share**.

Next to the name of the saved filter, there is a link to **Details**, which will allow you to edit the permissions:

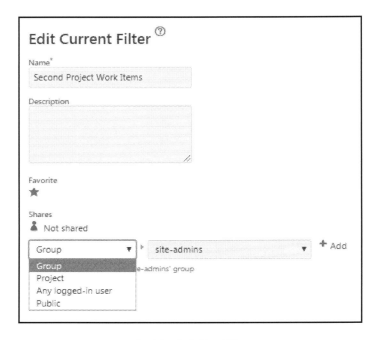

Permissions for the Current Filter

This allows us to set the permissions and subscriptions, and to see who should have access to them and should be able to see the contents of the filter. We have the ability to share this with a **Group**, a particular **Project**, **Any logged-in user**, or the **Public**. That's how we can save and manage our queries, and turn them into filters that other people can access and use.

Executing bulk changes

In this section, we'll discuss executing bulk changes. This can be really powerful when we need to make changes to many items, and we don't want to make those changes individually. We can do this by figuring out whether there is a pattern, or a way that we can make the change to many items. You're going to learn how to execute a bulk change by using the results of a filter.

In JIRA, let's take a look at one of our filters, as shown in the following screenshot. Looking at our **First Project Open Sprint Work Items** filter, we can see that it says project **FP1**, and, if the issue type is story, we're going to look at our open sprints and return everything ordered by the created date descending. It returns the two stories—**FP1-24** and **FP1-25**.

We want to change both of these stories to tasks. The best way to do this is with a bulk change; so, let's proceed. Go to the ellipsis in the upper right-hand corner, and click on **Bulk change all 2 issue(s)**:

Bulk change execution

This will bring us to the following screen:

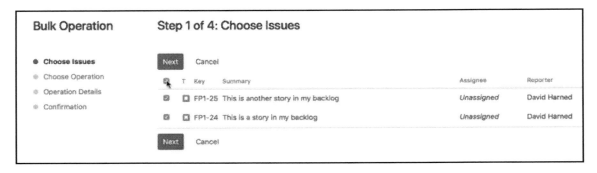

Bulk operation

Select the issues that you want to change, then click on **Next**. This will take you to the following screen:

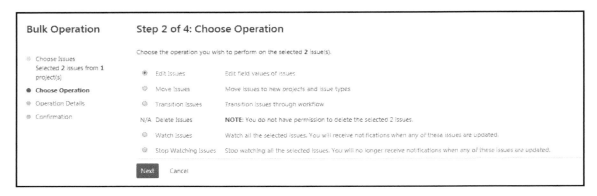

Choose the operation we would like to perform

We're going to choose the operation that we want to perform. We want to edit these issues, but we can also move them from one project to another, transition them to the workflow, and more. Let's select the **Edit Issues** option and then click on **Next**; then, we'll change the issue type to **Task**:

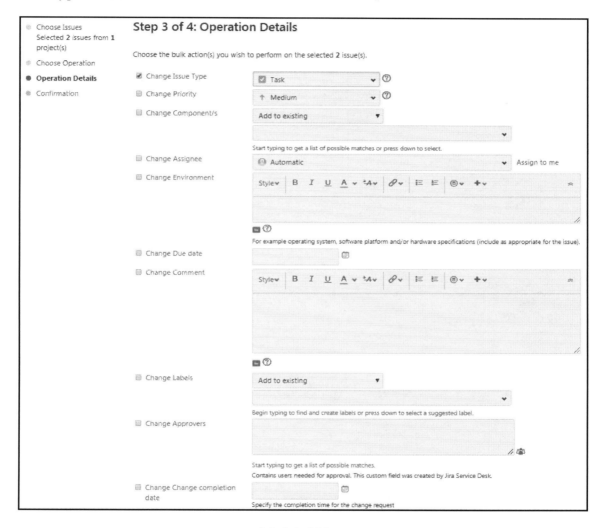

Define the detailed changes

As you can see in the preceding screenshot, we also have the ability to change lots of other attributes as well. We'll click on **Next** and then **Confirm**, as shown in the following screenshot:

It will go ahead and execute that change for us, as follows:

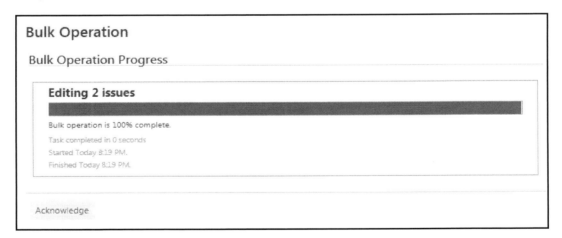

Bulk Operation execution

We'll let it run for a minute; when it's done, we can click on **Acknowledge**. If we go back to our query for this project issue type story, we won't get any results:

No results are found after the Bulk Operation completed

If we change the **IssueType** from Story to a `Task` and run this query again, we will see that we've changed these items from stories to tasks:

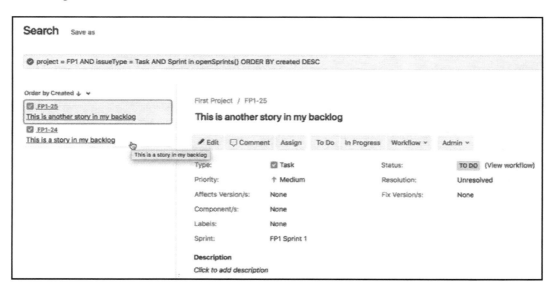

Running the updated query to confirm the bulk change

That's how we can execute a bulk change.

Creating new boards from saved filters

In this section, we'll cover creating new boards from saved filters. Here, we'll use a saved filter and create a new JIRA board from it. In the previous sections, we discussed JQL, creating a filter from a query, and bulk changes. Now, we're going to take a look at using the same filters to create a JIRA board.

As you can see in the following screenshot, we have a query. We've actually saved this query as a filter. Let's take a look at what this query does:

Saved filters

As shown in the preceding screenshot, it's basically returning all of the items in the **First Project** and **Second Project**, and it's ordering them by the creation date, descending. That's pretty simple; it's basically saying, show all of the work items in these two projects, in this specific order.

Let's use this to create a new board. Suppose that, hypothetically, we want to combine these two projects together into a bigger initiative, and we want to create a board that will let us view all of that in a single board view. We'll go over to the search menu, to **RECENT BOARDS**. Then, we'll click on **View all boards**:

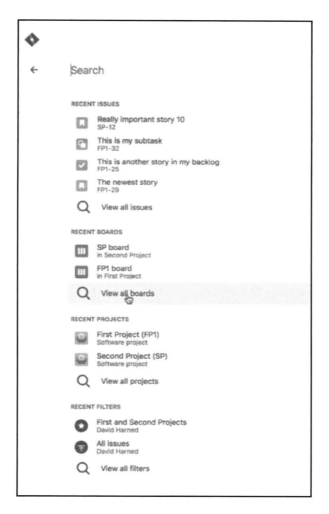

Viewing all boards from the search menu

A board automatically gets created when we create a new project. This is how you view the contents of the project. So, we can see that we actually have two boards already; we have the first project and the second project boards, as follows:

Here are all of our Boards. let's create new one

Now, we're going to create a new board. If we go to the upper right-hand corner, we can see a **Create board** option. Let's click on that. We'll get a prompt that gives us some options for what kind of board we'd like to create:

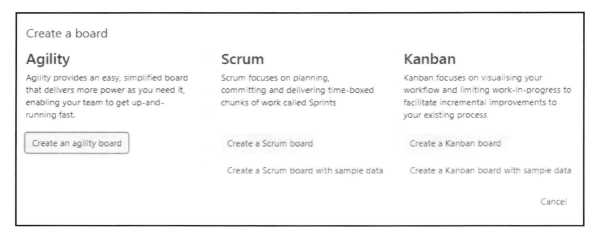

Options to Create a board

The first is the **Agility** board, which is the board that JIRA will create, to allow us to view the contents of a project in a more streamlined way. We already have projects in place with boards, so this isn't what we want. We're trying to create a board from a query. Next up is a **Scrum** board, which would include things like iterations; our current projects have these kinds of boards. We're really just trying to get a board view that gives us all of the contents of the two projects. **Kanban** is what we want to use in this situation. **Kanban** is really about moving items through a workflow and limiting the work in progress. Each column from left to right represents a step in the workflow. So, it will be a board with workflow columns that have the contents of our filter. Let's create a **Kanban** board.

In the following screenshot, we can see a few more options; for example, whether we want to create a new software project, an existing project, or a board from an existing saved filter:

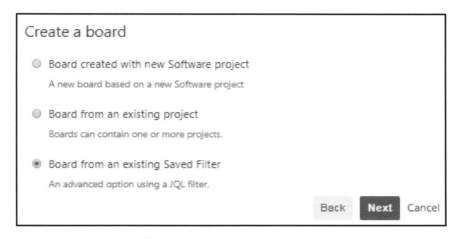

Create a board from our saved filter

Let's create a board by clicking on the **Board from an existing Saved Filter** option and clicking on **Next**. We'll give this a **Board name** of `All Projects`, and we'll use the **Saved Filter** called **First and Second Projects**. For the **Location** value, we can save this as another board underneath either the first or second projects, but let's just attach this to our profile, as shown in the following screenshot:

Name the board and assign a filter

Let's go ahead and create the board. We have a Kanban board with three columns—**TO DO**, **IN PROGRESS**, and **DONE**. All of the contents of both of the projects are on the board:

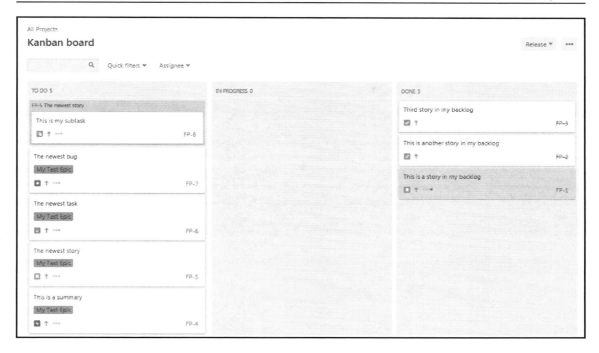

All Projects
Kanban board   Release ▾ •••

🔍   Quick filters ▾   Assignee ▾

TO DO 5	IN PROGRESS 0	DONE 3
FP-5 The newest story		Third story in my backlog
This is my subtask		☑ ↑ FP-3
☑ ↑ ••• FP-8		This is another story in my backlog
The newest bug		☑ ↑ FP-2
My Test Epic		This is a story in my backlog
☑ ↑ ••• FP-7		☑ ↑ • • FP-1
The newest task		
My Test Epic		
☑ ↑ ••• FP-6		
The newest story		
My Test Epic		
☑ ↑ ••• FP-5		
This is a summary		
My Test Epic		
☑ ↑ ••• FP-4		

Our new Board we made

Summary

In this chapter, you learned about JQL. Remember—here, it is not the Java Query Language, but the JIRA Query Language. You learned how to write simple and advanced queries using JQL, how to export query results, and how to save a query and turn it into a filter. Finally, you learned how to use saved filters to execute bulk changes, and how to use a saved filter to create a new JIRA board.

In our next (and final) chapter, we'll discuss dashboards and widgets.

6
Dashboards and Widgets

In this chapter, we'll discuss the dashboards and widgets in JIRA. We'll cover creating and managing dashboards, adding gadgets to dashboards, and sharing dashboards.

Dashboards broadcast how things are going and can share that information at a high level, being visible and transparent with regards to the results of the project.

In this chapter, we will cover the following topics:

- Creating and managing a dashboard
- Adding gadgets to a dashboard
- Sharing a dashboard

Creating and managing a dashboard

In this section, we'll cover creating and managing a dashboard. You're going to learn what a dashboard is, and how to create one.

Let's go to JIRA and take a look at some dashboards.

In our projects, we have the **First Project** and the **Second Project**; on the left-hand side, we can see **Dashboards**. JIRA comes with a **System dashboard** by default, so we can take a look at that in the following screenshot:

System dashboard—this is your default landing page

We can see an **Activity Stream** and some other items, but what we want to do is create our own dashboard; so, in the upper right-hand corner, click on the ellipses and go to **Create dashboard**. You'll see some options, where you can name the dashboard My Great Dashboard and give it a description—All the good things. We can start from a **Blank dashboard**, a **System dashboard**, or an existing one. We have a **Favorites** list, and we can mark our dashboard as a favorite in cases where there are many dashboards. We can also choose our sharing options, where we have the options such as to select a specific project, any logged in user, or public. For now, we'll just leave it in its default state:

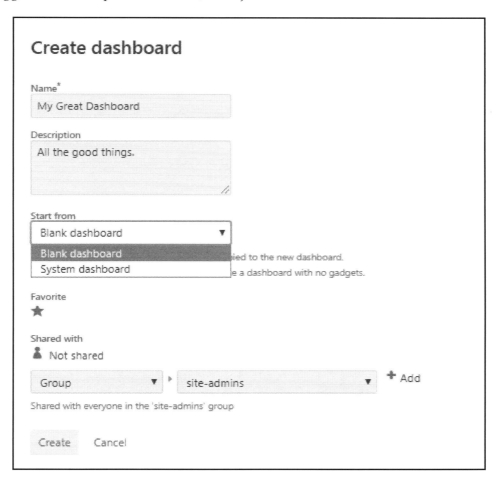

Creating a Blank dashboard

As you can see in the following screenshot, we've created our dashboard, where we can now add a new gadget:

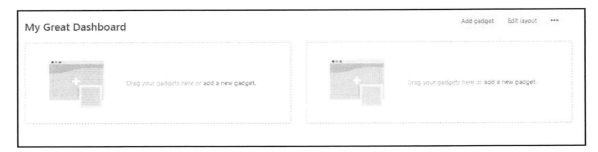

New dashboard's default state

Let's take a look at the layout options, as follows:

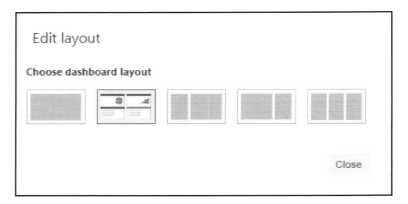

There are multiple dashboard layouts available

In the preceding screenshot, we can see one page that is like one giant chunk, where we can have multiple columns—a small column and a big one, the opposite of that, or three columns. It's up to us what we choose. We'll leave it at the default settings for now, but it's important that we know these options, so that we can share a dashboard that is configured in a way that's visually pleasing once we start to put these gadgets together.

Adding gadgets to our dashboard

In this section, we'll cover adding gadgets to our dashboard. You'll learn how to add the filter results gadget to a dashboard, as well as the pie chart gadget and the two-dimensional filter statistics. These are only a few of the options that are available. There are lots and lots of gadgets, but these are some of my favorites.

Let's go ahead and add some gadgets. Go back to JIRA; remember, we were dealing with **My Great Dashboard**, which we created in the last section.

There's something that you should know about gadgets. First of all, there are lots of them, and JIRA comes preloaded with quite a few. When we took a look at the Atlassian marketplace, there were about 95 different gadgets that were available for us to load into our dashboard, as well. There's even a gadget there to help us create our own gadgets! In addition to that, we can do things like reporting. This means that we can extend a dashboard quite a bit, in order to visualize all kinds of different things.

Let's take a look at the gadgets that we want to add. On our dashboard, we have a two-column layout. Let's click on **Add gadget**. This will take us to the following screen:

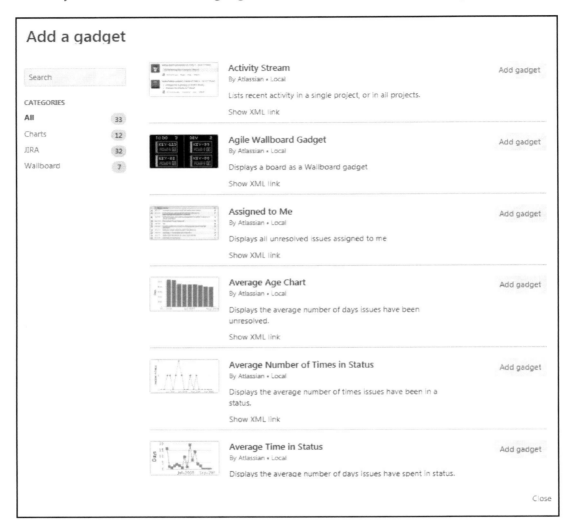

Gadgets available on JIRA to use

The first one that we're going to talk about is **Filter Results**. Let's type `filter` into the search box. Now, add the gadget by using the **Add gadget** button:

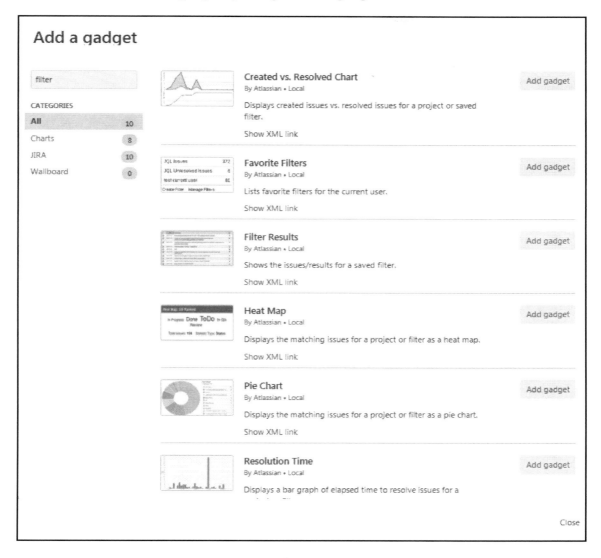

Addition of Filter Results gadget

We're also going to look for the pie chart, so we'll type in `pie`, and we'll add that gadget from the results, as follows:

Addition of Pie Chart gadget

Next, we'll get the **Two Dimensional Filter Statistics** gadget. Let's take a look at it:

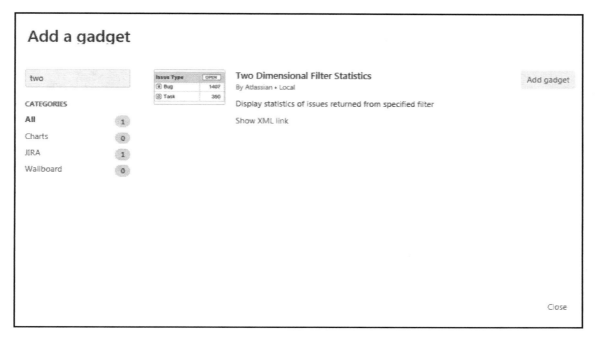

Adding the Two Dimensional Filter Statistics gadget

These are the three items that we're going to look at, but as you can see, we can keep adding them to our dashboard. The first thing that we will do is assign it a saved filter. Remember the **First and Second Project** filter that we made in a previous section when we created a board? That one returns the contents of the **First** and **Second** projects together, in one set of results. Let's use that one.

On our **XAxis**, we want to have the **Status** as horizontal access; this will be the status of all the work items. On the **YAxis**, we want to have the **Assignee**. We can change the **Sort By**, the **Sort Direction**, the **Number of Results**, and more. We can even set it to **Update every 15 minutes**, if we want to. We'll leave these at their defaults for now, and click on **Save**:

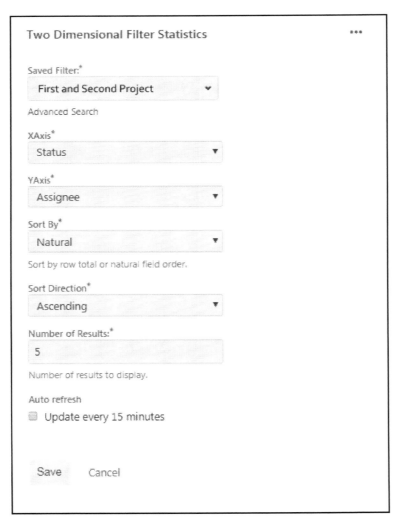

In the following screenshot, we can see our work items' **Status**, as well as what sprint they are in:

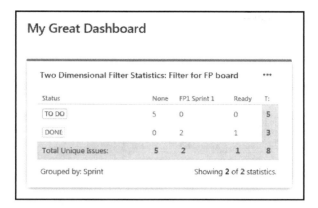

The other interesting thing about this chart is that we can actually click on the links of the counts in the cells; this will allow us to search for those issues. If we have a large team, this is a really good way of looking at the items for each person, and the state that they're in.

Next, let's take a look at the pie chart. We can do the same thing here; we can take a look at some of the filters and the projects that we have:

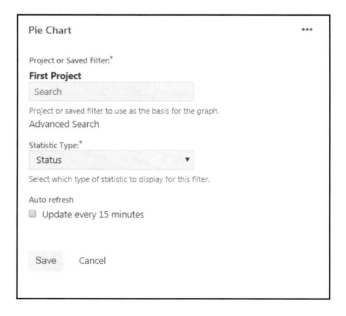

Let's take a look at what we have in the **First Project**, and keep the **Statistic Type** as **Status**. We'll hit **Save;** we can see that we now have a pie chart that shows the work **To Do** and **Done**:

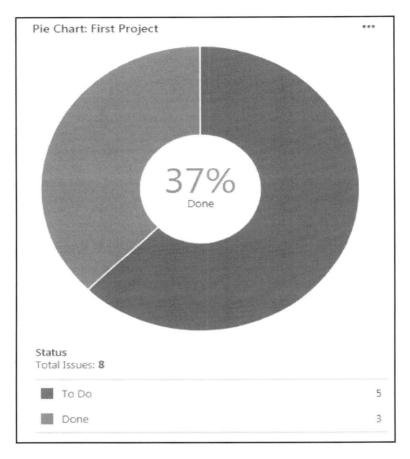

Pie Chart: First Project

37%
Done

Status
Total Issues: **8**

■	To Do	5
■	Done	3

If we have a large team, for example, we could look at how many people we have, how many work items we have, or even look at what the status of their work items was. Any number of things could be visualized using a pie chart.

Next, we're going to take a look at **Filter Results**. Again, let's assign a filter. We can pick the open sprint work items option. Again, we'll use the **First Project** items that are open. Here, we can have up to 10 results; we can choose the columns to display, and we can configure them or delete them. Let's go ahead and **Save** it:

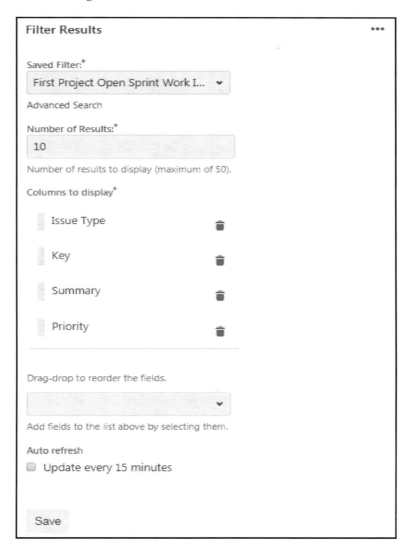

Let's go back to the edit screen and change the filter in order to look at the **Second Project**. We can select that filter and then display the contents as follows:

T	Key	Summary	P
		Filter Results: Filter for SP board	...
	SP-6	Really important story 5	↑
	SP-7	Really important story 8	↑
	SP-9	Really important story 7	↑
	SP-1	Test Story	↑
	SP-8	Really important story 6	↑
	SP-2	Really important story 1	↑
	SP-5	Really important story 4	↑
	SP-3	Really important story 2	↑
	SP-4	Really important story 3	↑
	SP-10	Really important story 9	↑

1–**10** of 11   1 2 ⟩

We can see the contents because we selected 10 items, and we're only seeing 10 of 12, but we can set that to as many as we want, as well as configure which columns show up.

These are three examples of gadgets on dashboards, but there are lots of different ones that we can choose from. In the next section, we'll discuss sharing our dashboard.

Sharing a dashboard

In this section, you'll learn how to share your dashboard. Remember, the whole concept of the dashboard is broadcasting results and making the results visible and transparent, so that's really what we're trying to do—make sure that everyone has access to them.

Let's head back to JIRA and take a look at the sharing settings for the dashboard. In the previous section, we created **My Great Dashboard**, and we gave it the contents that we can see in the following screenshot. We want to share this so that everyone can see it. Go to the ellipses in the upper right-hand corner and click on **Share dashboard**:

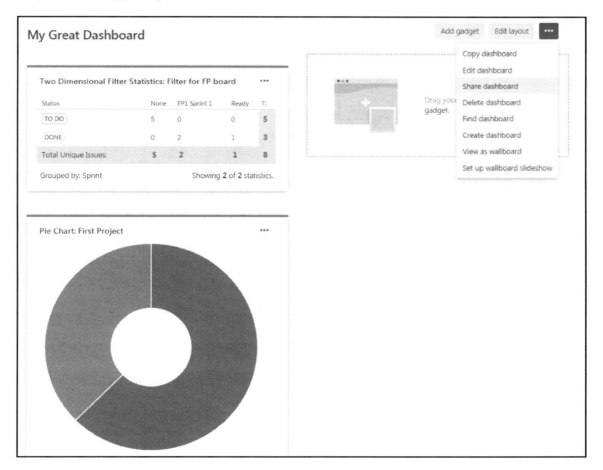

We also have lots of other options, but here, we're going to look at **Share**. We have the settings that we had when we originally set the dashboard up:

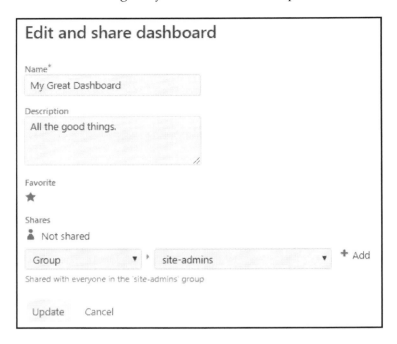

We can choose who can see the dashboard; we can even make it **Public**. We can see that this page states that sharing with the public will make this visible to everyone including users who are not logged in; if we want our customers or someone else to be able to see the dashboard, this is a nice option. We can also click on **Update** and share it with them that way. Otherwise, we can choose anyone on the project, and then select which project, and more. This is how we can share our dashboard.

Summary

In this chapter, we covered how to create a dashboard, how to add gadgets to a dashboard by using the filters that we created, and how to share a dashboard with others, making the results transparent and visible.

This brings us to the end of our time together with JIRA. I hope that you have found this dive into JIRA useful and that you are able to take what you have learned and apply it to your specific scenarios. Thank you for spending this time with me. Do you have additional questions? Please look me up on social media and ask away! Good luck with your projects.

Other Books You May Enjoy

If you enjoyed this book, you may be interested in these other books by Packt:

Jira Software Essentials - Second Edition
Patrick Li

ISBN: 9781788833516

- Understand the basics and agile methodologies of Jira software
- Use Jira Software in a Scrum environment
- Manage and run Jira Software projects beyond the out of box Scrum and Kanban way
- Combine Scrum and Kanban and use other project management options beyond just agile
- Customize Jira Software's various features and options as per your requirements
- Work with Jira Agile offline, and plan and forecast projects with an agile portfolio
- Integrate Jira Agile with Confluence and Bitbucket

JIRA 7 Administration Cookbook - Second Edition
Patrick Li

ISBN: 9781785888441

- Customize basic settings for your projects, such as screens and fields
- Create and customize workflows to suit your business process needs
- Make workflows more effective and efficient
- Manage users and groups inside JIRA and manage advanced login options
- Secure your JIRA instance using effective practices
- Perform e-mail functionalities with JIRA
- Extend JIRA to integrate with other products and services

Leave a review - let other readers know what you think

Please share your thoughts on this book with others by leaving a review on the site that you bought it from. If you purchased the book from Amazon, please leave us an honest review on this book's Amazon page. This is vital so that other potential readers can see and use your unbiased opinion to make purchasing decisions, we can understand what our customers think about our products, and our authors can see your feedback on the title that they have worked with Packt to create. It will only take a few minutes of your time, but is valuable to other potential customers, our authors, and Packt. Thank you!